FARRAR
STRAUS
GIROUX

Coyote v. Acme

Coyote v. Acme

[Ian Frazier]

Farrar, Straus and Giroux

New York

Printed in the United States of America

Published simultaneously in Canada by HarperCollins*CanadaLtd*

First edition, 1996

Library of Congress Cataloging-in-Publication Data

Frazier, Ian.

Coyote v. Acme / Ian Frazier.—1st ed.

p.   cm.

I. Title.

PN6162.F729   1996   814′.54—dc20   95-26360 CIP

These pieces appeared originally in *The New Yorker*,
The Atlantic Monthly, and *Army Man*.

To Saul Steinberg

Contents

Coyote v. Acme

The Last Segment

At a signal from the sound room, the tapes stopped spinning, and one by one the big thousand-watt lights winked and darkened. Then Mary hugged Murray, and Ted came over and hugged them both, and then Lou, usually so uncomfortable with physical displays, took all three in a bear hug that had them gasping for breath through their tears. Then Grant came onto the set and announced that he had bought each of them an Arabian pony, which they could ride whenever they wanted. Then from someplace offstage two technicians came in carrying—literally carrying—Sue Ann. She had been so cheerful all day, but when she happened to see "MARY TYLER MOORE SHOW CAN-CELLED" in black-and-white in a newspaper headline, the full reality finally hit her, and she collapsed. Members of the live audience were weeping and calling out the names of their favorites, but security guards standing three-deep kept all but the most persistent behind the front rail. Thousands more waited outside in the rain to pay their respects to executive producer Stan Daniels; one at a time they were admitted, given a few seconds, and ushered out. The representative from Courier-brand tub and tile cleaner provided a cake seven tiers high (one tier for each season on the network), decorated with the titles of every episode and topped with exact replicas of the main characters whittled from basswood by an old man from the Ozarks whom Murray had met while driving cross-country. Ted and Lou, who had never been much closer off camera than on, stood staring down at the buffet table, side by side. When Ted turned and haltingly offered Lou the blazer he had worn on the show since the beginning, both men's shoulders began to shake, and they sobbed openly. Then Mary made a speech. She told everybody that she loved them and would always remember them, and if they ever felt they needed her, all they had to do was think of her and she would be there. Then she repeated the whole speech in fluent sign language, her hands trembling slightly in the waning light.

Then the staff carpenters, working with a delicacy all the more touching in such burly men, dismantled the sets and loaded them into trucks for immediate removal to the Smithsonian Institution, where they would one day be put on permanent display. The air grew heavy with the scent of diesel exhaust and leave-taking as men from the telephone company seized fire axes and began chopping away the cables. Like the wings of giant birds coming to earth, the microwave towers slowly fell. The instant that groundwater reached the boiler room, four-inch rivets started to pop and fly across the now flaming studio. Heedless of the chaos around them, members of the original cast swayed together with their arms still entwined, their eyes distant and glazed with trance. Later they would describe how they had been transported to a faraway land where they met and conversed with the stars from every program that had ever been aired, who told them not to be downcast but to rejoice. The house orchestra played every number it knew, ending with one last rendition of the famous theme song just as dawn was breaking. The entire company watched from a nearby knoll as the lot filled with ash until only the flagpole remained; then that, too, was gone. Finally, as if waking from a dream that still held them in its grip, they made their way toward the ranks of limousines waiting to take them back to the world they'd left behind, to the people they used to be.

·

Little brother was never quite right after that, and in the fall he was sent away. Mama doesn't make big Sunday dinners like she did before; mostly she just calls Meals on Wheels. There was a virus going around, Papa caught it, and he died last spring. Sister married a soldier and moved to Toledo. At the old home place, only Cousin Eleanor remains. Sometimes in the evenings she tries to sit in the front room, but it's no use. There was little to keep Lloyd around any longer, so he went back on the road. At an icy intersection in a distant state, a semi-trailer full of salt blocks overturned on him, it'll be two years ago this Christmas. The other Lloyd, the one Nancy married, escaped into his work, and drove his cherry picker against some high-tension wires not twenty minutes after attending a safety lecture sponsored by the power company. With weekday attendance down, Grandy just couldn't keep the inn running the way it used to, and he had to sell out to the Flammia brothers. They stripped the furnishings and put in a snack-meats factory. Curtis figured that he might as well have the operation; he seems fine now. His wife, while admiring his courage, nevertheless felt she had no choice but to file for divorce. Trestle still takes his strolls down Main Street, but his conversation dwells increasingly on the past. Mark became a pharmacist. Galen is presumed missing. Bev traded what she could never have for what she'd never wanted in the first place, and married Chick. They shut down the pool hall, they shut down the Grange hall, they filled in the swimming hole and put a Substance Abuse Center where the old gazebo used to be. And see the tree, how big it's grown; beneath, a simple marker, with the words "Home by Midnight" and the familiar five-pointed star of a Texas Ranger. Afternoons now, Wade stacks change in piles according to size, dreaming away behind the drive-thru window. The children are long gone, vanished into sports and other outside interests. Somewhere, invisible pens compute the swirling arithmetic of loss.

·

And me? I'm sitting in a bar in Gander, Newfoundland, wondering how I ever got so far from that old gravel road that runs past the fields of my memories. When I look back at the happiness I knew, it appears to me now as if through the wrong end of a

telescope—tiny, remote, yet precise in every detail.
I remember how we all used to assemble at the couch
at five minutes to nine, each of us well supplied with
blankets and refreshments to insure that we wouldn't
have to budge for the next half hour. And how long
those ads seemed in between! Sometimes we would
joke about the "idiot box," the "vast wasteland." We
didn't know what a wasteland was. Seems like ever
since the cancellation I just can't put those times far
enough behind me. Measure the distance by airports,
pay phones, hotels, cities, women. Sure, there've
been women—plenty of them. I'm not ashamed of
their number, because it was from them I learned how
much hurt there is in the world, and how much
gentleness.

A while back a buddy of mine wrote to say that I
should come home. Beneath his words I sensed a
wistful tone, as if the person he was trying hardest to
convince was himself. Of course, I had to say no. He
may think that my refusal means I have no hope. In
fact, the opposite is closer to the truth. For in spite
of all I've been through, I find that I still believe in
human beings. I just do. To pretend to enjoy the
formulaic treatments of today would be to deny that.
For seven years, an entire nation sat down as one,
week after week, to watch a miracle. I know in my
heart that it will happen again—maybe not next fall,
or the fall after that, but someday. When it does, no
one will have to ask me to come home, because wherever on the globe I may happen to be, I'll be home
already.

From the Bank

with Your Money

on Its Mind

Dear Depositor:

Last quarter marked the beginning of an exciting cash-management policy here at First Tri-State Drive-Thru Banking & Trust. Under our new "Money Mover" system, we've started reassigning cash from the accounts of people it belongs to and getting it on the "move." As you know, money that just sits around actually loses value, and must be cared for the way you would care for any helpless thing. And that means time lost, opportunities missed, and vacations postponed—some, perhaps, indefinitely. We know how hard you work for your money, and that's why it will always be welcome here. In return, your money will give us a chance to do what we do best, not only for ourselves but also for the benefit of our families and the many people who serve them.

Depositors with an interest in the smaller details of bank routine may wish to refer to the explanatory list of letter codes at the end of their statement. If we can assist in any way with inquiries about the "Money Mover" system or your statement, feel free to call the

24-hour toll-free depositors' hot-line telephone number, which we have recently given out to several people. (Please do not call the bank.)

> Yours sincerely,
> DOUG & DAVE FLAMMIA
> Co-Chairmen,
> First Tri-State

First Tri-State Drive-Thru Banking & Trust

STATEMENT OF ACCOUNT

Acc't Name:

Kevin J. Kopenhaver
1085 Overlook Court, Apt. 5

Savings Acc't. Number	Previous Balance	Deposits	Withdrawals, Debits, and Other Charges	Present Balance
3-17-411	23,718.00	1,600.00	25,311.27	6.73

—Deposits—

Date	Amount	Date	Amount
3/15	400.00 DP	5/16	400.00 DP
4/19	400.00 DP	6/14	400.00 DP

—Withdrawals, Debits, and Other Charges—

Date	Amount	Date	Amount
3/18	4.80 APC	4/26	1,075.00 MDD
3/19	10.00 BMC	4/30	3,500.00 N-N-N'N-N
3/22	10.00 CS	5/3	750.00 O!S
3/25	6.75 CTF	5/8	299.00 O,DTBBWHLPB
3/28	1,148.80 E,U	5/13	238.36 P,YBMH
4/5	95.25 AR	5/14	6.00 PCC
4/8	520.00 HT,PF	5/22	585.00 SW
4/11	1,000.00 LDP	5/27	972.23 SKYMIAS,C
4/12	282.25 GRA	6/3	2,000.00 TL,B
4/16	75.65 FC	6/7	895.80 WGMM
4/17	122.00 KNI	6/12	2,000.00 TASM
4/19	325.50 IFIG	6/13	5,888.88 Y—SW
4/23	1,625.00 MYOB	6/14	1,875.00 YAWA

CODES:

APC	Applied to Previous Charges	MYOB	Mind Your Own Business
AR	Cash Advance Reversal	N-N-N'N-N	Nya-Nya-N'Nya-Nya
BMC	Billing Memo Charge	O,DTBBWHLPB	Oh, Does the Big Baby Want
CS	Charge for Service		His Little Pennies Back?
CTF	Credit Transfer Fee	O!S	Ooops! Sorry
DM	Debit Memo	PCC	Print Check Charge
DP	Deposit	P,YBMH	Please, You're Breaking
E,U	Error, Unavoidable		My Heart
FC	Finance Charge	SKYMIAS,C	So Keep Your Money in a
GRA	Growth Rate Adjustment		Sock, Crybaby
HT,PF	Head Teller, Pocket Funds	SW	Says Who?
IFIG	Insufficient Funds in General	TASM	Try and Stop Me
KNI	Kathy Needed It	TL,B	Tough Luck, Buster
LDP	Liquidity Depletion Prepayment	WGMM	Who's Gonna Make Me?
MC	Miscellaneous Charge	Y—SW	Yeah—So What?
MDD	My Dog Died	YAWA	You and What Army?

From the Bank

Confused about sex? Maybe what you need is the help of your own personal banker. Now, as a special service to First Tri-State Drive-Thru customers, Doug and Dave Flammia are offering their practical booklets "When to Pet, When Not to: A Guide for Young Investors," "Estate Planning in an Era of Sexual Change," "Some Straight Talk About IRAs and Sex," and "Swimsuit Photos of the Very Rich," all for just six dollars a set. Send cash only to FlammiArt, Inc., Box 1611, Radio City Station, New York, N.Y. 10101. Residents of U.S. please add 73¢ postage and handling.

Webbing

"What's come over Janine, anyway?" Stu asks, reaching for the Chianti. He is sitting at the umbrella table on the patio, reading an article in the Sunday magazine section ("Milton Friedman, Economist for the Ages," June 17th, page 32). I am sitting at the edge of the pool, dangling my feet and looking at the way the water makes my shins appear to bend a little bit forward. We are at my mother's third husband's summer house on Long Island, approximately a ninety-minute drive from New York City.

Stu looks at me, but I don't answer. Janine is his stepsister, and, to tell the truth, I have always found her disturbing. Stu knows that; after a moment, he fills his glass and returns to his magazine. Since Stu is in advertising, being employed by Miles & McMullan, on Sixty-fourth Street, he loves to look at the ads. He turns the pages smoothly, as if the magazine were an extension of himself.

From the portable radio sitting on the cocktail cart, the latest hit song blares:

Webbing

She's ferocious,
And she knows just what it takes
  to make a pro blush . . .

"Earth calling Pam! Earth calling Pam!" Nat startles me. Nat has come onto the patio through the sliding glass doors while I was lost in my reverie. Nat is Stu's best friend from Bennington, in Vermont, and my former lover. Actually, he was my lover, then he was my former lover, then he was my lover again, and now he's my former lover again. (Stu knows nothing of this.) Nat is a carpenter, and a good one. His hands caressing the grain of fine wood furniture have a beauty all their own. Stu and I are being gentle with Nat these days, because his grandmother just died. Not his real grandmother but a regional sales representative for True Temper Hardware, whom Nat used to call Grandmother. Nat's lady, Alice, is in the hospital having a baby this morning, so Nat has both death and birth in his life.

From the Sony portable television in the cabaña, the happy jingle of a tuna-fish commercial can be heard:

Yum-Yum Bumble Bee
Bumble Bee Tuna.
I love Bumble Bee
Bumble Bee Tuna

I look at Nat over my sunglasses. "Hi, Nat," I say. "Wrong again. Nat's gone to the station to pick up

Claudette," Jerry says. Jerry is Nat's identical-twin brother, as well as a skilled potter.

"Jerry . . ." Stu says, reaching for an apple. "You didn't invite Claudette up here? Did you?"

"Well, I kind of did, actually," Jerry says, scanning the distant tree line. Claudette is a sculptor, and a Hawaiian. Stu knows I find Hawaiians very troubling.

On the television, on "The Magilla Gorilla Show," Magilla is trying to explain something to Mr. Peebles, the pet-store owner.

Suddenly, a memory of when I was a little girl comes to me, vaulting over the years as fresh and vivid as if it happened yesterday. One Sunday in June, when I was ten or eleven, my father (or was it my older brother; no, it was my father, I'm pretty sure) —anyway, he took me and my friend Kathy, or, rather, Beverly, in our car down Route 632 and we drove to Forster's and we got frozen custard. Either that or maybe we went to the park.

There is a crunch of gravel in the driveway. A minute later, Nat, Claudette, Aida, and René come through the hedge. Aida and René are two other people whom we know. Almost telepathically, I can feel Stu start to worry. For his sake, and for the sake of the life he has so carefully imagined for us, I smile up at them all. The look of terror on Nat's face freezes my greeting in my throat.

"Krauts!" Nat screams, tackling Claudette to the terrazzo and shielding her body with his own as the deafening blast of jet engines fills the air and twin .50-calibre machine guns stitch the wood siding above him into a splintered needlepoint of death.

"Hit the dirt!" Stu cries, but I am way ahead of him, hugging the concrete so fiercely as to weld its very soul to mine.

In the next few moments, total pandemonium takes over. Explosions are everywhere. The earth beneath me lifts and falls. *Whomp! Whomp!* Troops run by carrying rockets and mortars. Theirs or ours? I cannot tell. Ricocheting bullets sting my cheek with spurts of pulverized brick dust. Am I screaming? I must be; the universe is one endless scream, and I am part of it. More guys run by with guns and radios. One horrible thought fills my entire mind: *America is being invaded! And by Germans!* The staccato burst of a machine gun stutters out its fatal message as tracer bullets set the garden ablaze. How can it be? We defeated the Germans soundly over forty years ago! But it's true—I knew the moment the plane came over on its strafing run and I smelled that familiar Boche smell (not familiar to me, of course, because I was too young for WW II; I mean familiar to my father, who told me about it)—that smell of ether, camel dung, and boiled cabbage that the German Army carried wherever it went.

"Move out! To the trees! It's our only chance!" Nat shouts, as the rain of spent shell casings on the tile roof sounds a grim counterpoint to his hoarse command. There is a brief lull in the firing, like a rest in a famous symphony, and then all hell breaks loose again and we are on our feet, suddenly, and running. Running blindly, running and crawling and dodging through a world of fresh craters newly in bloom with orange orchids of smoky flame. Just then, I happen to look up at the trees we are running toward, only to see them begin to topple to one side and another —an entire division of Panzer tanks, heading straight for us! With the energy born of desperation, I grab a German paratrooper who has just landed, hit him with a karate chop on the bridge of the nose, and wrestle his submachine gun away. Throwing myself flat in one of the nearby craters, I begin pumping round after round into the approaching ranks of the invader, as a brassy taste I know to be fear fills my parched and tightening throat.

.

When I was in the fourth grade—when I was nine years old, and ten—I sometimes used to wonder if somewhere on earth there might not be another little girl who was exactly like me in every way, who looked like me and dressed like me and talked like me and had the same barrettes and everything. And what if we went to the same school—who would be the more popular, she or I? Then, too, I used to wonder what I would do if I had a million dollars, and which movie star I would like to marry, and who would win if God and Superman got into a fight, and which horse was prettier, Misty of Chincoteague or National Velvet, and whether ballerinas had to do gym at school or could get excused. I guess every kid wonders about stuff like that. Now that I am grown, with a husband and a wife and children of my own, I can see that many of the questions I used to wonder about, while not wrong, were certainly misguided. All of us—

friends, lovers, colleagues, German troopers—are usually caught up in a scheme much larger than we imagine at the time. It's just like the webbing of the lawn chair I was sitting near right before the attack: to us, our lives seem to be straight lines, but in fact they are interwoven with other lives in a way that makes a net, or web, that maybe some greater being might use for something, just in the way we use that lawn chair. Nat loves me; I love Stu; Stu loves Claudette; Claudette loves Mr. Hurstwood (from *Sister Carrie*, by Theodore Dreiser). Weaving and reweaving, these many separate strands seek their own warp and woof. To me, it is all quite astonishing. This raid by combined German air and ground forces only serves to underscore my point.

Boswell's Life

of Don Johnson

To attempt to preserve for posterity one whose wit and understanding outsped the swiftest minds in his business, and who knew better than any other the temper of his age and time slot, is a task for which any honest man must declare himself unfit. That Don Johnson should receive no chronicler approaching himself in stature is, I fear, a condition necessarily imposed by the eminence of his person. On my behalf, I present as credentials only a lively affection for my subject, coupled with a respect for the lofty qualities of his imagination—inclinations grown many times greater in the course of an intimacy that endured, to my gratification, through a period of several weeks' time.

As a young man raised in Scotland, and later (after a reversal in my family's fortunes) in a Thrifty Scot motel, I longed for the intellectual pleasures of the metropolis. Like many others throughout Europe and the Americas whose interest in the arts and sciences no provincial seat could satisfy, I filled my leisure hours with fancies of Miami, Florida. And, naturally, with every thought of Miami came thoughts of Don Johnson, whose name with Miami's shall be forever

linked, and whose reputation shines as the brightest
ornament of the location where he tapes. Accordingly,
when I attained my majority I removed to that city,
and settled myself in rented beachfront lodgings
within walking distance of the Seaquarium.

•

My friend having but little interest in reviewing for
me the smaller details of his birth and upbringing, I
must rely for this account upon remarks that I think
I heard him make at one meeting or another. Don
Johnson was born near the midpoint of his century to
a couple who also lived in that time. Like many young
boys, Don Johnson was inclined to mischief. His parents either wished him to read law at university in
preparation for a career at the bar or else they did
not wish it or else they had no thoughts on the matter.
For his own part, when his schooling was finished, or
earlier, Don Johnson strengthened his resolve to brave
the uncertainties of a player's life. Toward this end,
he changed his probable Christian name, "Donald,"
to the better and more dramatic "Don."

•

My own introduction to Don Johnson was an occasion
of such moment that I refrain from entrusting it to
memory's leaky barque. Instead, I refer to an entry
made shortly afterward in my daily breviary:

March 11
Dined this evening in company at Enrique's Little Havana,
an eating place (with dancing). Of a sudden, came a mea-

sure of stirring music, and through the door strode a man
of good figure and erect carriage, wearing a light-colored
nankeen suit and spectacles of a tint so opaque as to hide
the eyes within. Instantly, I recognized the celebrated Don
Johnson—this despite his stature, which was in appearance somewhat shorter than in the portrait at the National
Gallery. At the first opportunity, I took leave of my party,
made my way to his table, and, emboldened by the warmth
of my sentiment, clasped him by the hand. Conveying to
him my admiration in the strongest terms, I added that I
had many questions that I hoped one day to discuss with
him, and inquired whether I might call upon him some
afternoon at his trailer. In the silence that ensued, my
heart raced in anticipation of another of Don Johnson's
famed epigrams, when, with a look at his companions
at table, Don Johnson replied, "Hey. Who *is* this wing
nut?"

Later, I was to learn that my friend's abruptness
bespoke no hidden depths of ill-humor but only the
natural impatience of a spirited intellect checked by
society's custom. Indeed, when next we met, and I,
blushing crimson and stammering out my words, yet
managed to ask of him whether he did all his own
stunts, he responded most willingly. I then followed
by inquiring how he contrived to juggle his fame with
his personal life, and so began a conversation that
continued late into the evening.

To those several critics who, with but the most
superficial knowledge, accuse Don Johnson of haughty
and peremptory behavior, I reply that my friend has

long suffered from a recurring melancholia, brought on by the exigencies of a career that no critic could ever sustain. In addition, I submit that Don Johnson became (through no fault of his own) a man of painfully divided loyalties: on the one hand, he belonged to the city, while, on the other hand, he belonged to the night. We can only imagine the agonies of doubt this must have occasioned within him, as his mind turned first toward the one indebtedness, and then toward the other. Moreover, Don Johnson has been troubled at irregular intervals by a very rare disorder whereby the reflections of street lamps cross the lenses of his spectacles in dizzying succession and deafening airs from popular operettas fill his ears. That he has managed even the smallest degree of civility in the face of such impediments I consider a remarkable feat.

Recently, I found among my papers the text of a hymn that, though unsigned, shows the unmistakable evidence of Don Johnson's authorship. As I recall, it was composed as a tribute to his friend Lord Cranwyck, of Ayles, Lincolnshire, in celebration of the latter's marriage to a mutual friend. It reads, in part:

> You did it, pal—hey, it's a lock.
> You got legs, Mister; you can walk.
> The gig's a tough one, understand?
> Count on it, buddy—ask the man.
> Pal, get the wax out of your ears.
> We're lookin' at at least ten years.
> The only thing I'm gonna say—
> Hey, read my lips: "Flight's cancelled, Ray."

Were Don Johnson's detractors only aware of this and many other proofs of devotion which he showed repeatedly to those cherished in his affection, I am certain they would revise their opinions.

On the subject of women, Don Johnson is perhaps best known for his remark that whereas one cannot, assuredly, live with them, one cannot, by equal measure, live without them. Of his own version of marriage, to a daughter of the French-sounding D'Arbanville family, I shall speak more at a later time. Suffice it to say that Don Johnson had the wisdom to choose for a companion an actress whose beauty, charm, talent, and sense of fun all vie with each other for preference in the eye of the observer, and one who can do an excellent imitation of a person coughing. I seem to recall hearing recently that Don Johnson and Patti had moved to separate dwellings; however, I believe someone else possibly informed me (more recently yet) that they were once again together, which later report I hope may be fact, inasmuch as I think she is nice.

perfect place? The trunk of a 1975 brown Buick LeSabre in a deserted area of the Mill Basin section of Brooklyn! From a fifty-gallon drum at the bottom of the Gulf of sunny Mexico, to the foundations of the art-deco-inspired Chrysler Building, in Manhattan, to a shallow mound of fresh earth in Rambouillet Forest, southwest of romantic Paris, every successful party requires but one ingredient: people. A dear friend of mine in a field behind her house in Leeds, just 150 feet from her front door, once said to me, "Elsa—" Of course I sympathized completely. All of us may feel a bit apprehensive when we contemplate giving a big social affair. The first thing I do is make a list—something like:

> planter's punch
> crepe-paper streamers
> Nancy and Henry Kissinger
> a crawl space
> four twenty-gallon plastic bags
> pretty girls
> gladiolas by the armful
> a remote fishing-access site
> Bobby Short

Now that I've got the basic outline, I can relax and let my imagination color it in.

As I once remarked to Consuelo Vanderbilt in an unclaimed crate at the International Arrivals Building at Kennedy Airport, money and titles mean nothing to me. Character, sense of humor, charm, and dental

Where the Bodies

Are Buried

At long last, the glamorous and poignant saga of Elsa
Maxwell is coming to a bookshop near you. . . . "Party
Girl: The Elsa Maxwell Story" by Rosemary Kent. . . .
"Elsa knew where the bodies were buried," said Kent.
—William Norwich, in the New York *Daily News*

You're at an intimate dinner party. The guest on your
left is under the blacktop driveway of a two-bedroom
brick house in Highland Park, Michigan. How do you
begin a conversation? I'm a firm believer in the old
rule that one must always avoid politics and religion
at the dinner table. Try instead to draw your companion out on subjects of general interest—boarded-
up closets, for example. Even the dullest guest is
likely to have some thoughts about them. If that fails
to strike a spark, try air shafts. Chances are, you'll
be talking away in no time. If it's a summer party,
how about air-conditioning vents? Or, if you happen
to be dining outside, the topic of wooded areas might
be promising. If none of these seem to appeal, put
on your brightest smile and turn to the guest on your
right. After all, you've done your best.

What's the perfect time for a party? Any time! The

records are what I look for in a guest. To me, a county landfill project full of dukes and millionaires is a county landfill project full of bores. At any gathering it's the mix of personalities that makes things go. If I invite a person from the A list, I make sure to include one from the B list, one from the world of show business, one from a creek in the Bronx, one from the arts, one from a storm drain in Great Neck, and so forth. A varied crowd guarantees your party against the horrors of shop talk.

People often ask me, "Is it permissible to wear evening clothes to a gathering in the late afternoon?" "On which side of the salad fork should one place the posthole digger and scrap-metal compactor?" "Is a commercial strength of quicklime sufficient for my entertaining needs?" "Should I require my caterer to provide an estimate in advance?" "What's in the chimney of the pharmacy on North Lincoln Avenue?" "How many cinder blocks should I allow for each unescorted woman?" "What about the narrow passageway separating the building at 684 Ralph Avenue from the adjoining building?" "What is that odd smell?" "Should I examine a double-locked steamer trunk mailed slow freight to a nonexistent address in New Orleans?" "Should I check the refuse bins of a popular theme park? The hold of a burned fishing boat off Craig, Alaska? A vacant lot on Dean Street, between Classon and Grand avenues? A rented room on West Seventy-sixth Street? The bottom of an elevator shaft in an Ozone Park housing project? The tall grass at the entry to the Hutchinson River Parkway near

Bruckner Boulevard? Beneath the paving stones in the courtyard of the Via Veneto restaurant in Queens? In the wall of the men's room of a Brooklyn veterans' meeting hall? Under the service bay of a derelict garage in Keansburg, New Jersey?"

I always answer, "Warmer, warmer. Yes, my dears, you are getting warmer all the time."

Brandy by Firelight

. . . she had a laugh that was like brandy by firelight.
—Something I read somewhere

Courvoisier VSOP. Burning garden shed. "Hee-hee *yuk* yuk-yuk-yuk-yuk-yuk-yuk!"

Rémy Martin Napoleon. Kitchen grease fire. "Har har har, ha ha harr harr harr harr harr harrrrr!"

Cordon Bleu Martell. Torched kerosene-soaked rags. "Whee-ha-ha-ha h'h'h' h'h'hee oh-ho-hoh he he he he he he he he he he!"

Mercier Prestige. Overheated car engine. "Ya-hah-ha-ha-ha. Ya-ha-ha-ha-ha. Yah-ha-ha-ha-ha."

Hennessy XO. Old telephone books on electric space heater. "Hih-hih-hih, hih-hih-hih, oh ho ho ho ho ho, yee-hoo hoo hoo ha ho ho ho, uh-heh, uh-heh, ha ha ha HA HA HA heh heh heh heh heh heh heh!"

Ragnaud Reserve Special. Southern California brush-fire. "Ya-*hoo* ha ha ha ha ha ha whoop! ha ha ha ha ha ha whee-ha hoo-*ee!* ha ha ha *uh*-oh! ho ho ho hee hee hee oh ho ho ho hee hee hee ch'k ch'k."

Felipe II. Chinese-food cartons at bottom of ventilator shaft. "A-hah, a-hah, a-HAH HAH HAHHH, a-HAH-HAH-HAH HAH-HAH HAHHHH HAHHHHH HAHHHHH HAHH-HHHHHHH HAHHHHHHHHHH-HHHHHHHHHHHHHH, a-hah, HAHHHHH HAHHHHH HAH HA, a-hah, a-hah a-hah!"

Château des Plasson VSOP. Abandoned wood-frame summer cottage. "P-p-p-p-*pah!* ha ha HA HA HAAA HAAA-A-A-A-A-A HA HA HA HOO HOO HOO HOO HOO HOO HOO HOO HEE HEE HEE HEE huh huh A-*HEE* HEE HEE HEE HEE HEE HEE HEE HEE HEE uh huh uh huh HEE HEE HEE HEE WHEE-HEE HEE HEE a-hee a-hee a-hee a-hah HOO HOO HOO HOO HOO HOO HEE HEE HEE HEE!"

Slivovitz Old Plum. Lit match in the stuff between subway rails. "A-hilk a-hilk a har har har hilk hilk hilk hilk hilk hilk hilk hilk."

Fundador. Butane lighter at thirty thousand feet. "Hee hee hee ya-hah-hah-hah ho ho whee-ha ho ho hee-ya hah hah WHOO-HOO-HOO-HOO-HOO oh-hohk, hack, hack, a, HEE HEE HEE HEE HEE HEEEE, oh-hohk, HACK! *HACK!* a-HOO HOO HOO HOO HEEE HACK! *HACK!*"

Christian Brothers. Tasselled restaurant-menu cord in candle flame. "A-ssshaw haw haw haw sheee haw haw haw."

Rémy Martin Louis XIII. Offshore-oil platform. "Ah-hah hah hah hee hee hee whhooooooeeeeeee hee hee hee hee hee oh *plea-hee-hee-hee-hee-se* hoo hoo hoo hee hee hee gimme a break hoo hoo hoo you're killin' me hee hee hee hee no stop please wha-he-ha-hah-hah-hah-hah-hah HOOOOO HEEEEE HA HA HA HA HA HA HO HO HO HO HO HO HOO HO HO HO oh man too much! HEE HEE HEE HEE HO HO HO HO HO HO HO HO HO HO HO HO HA HA, a,hah, a,hah, a,hah, a,hah I'm *dyin'* hee hee hee hee hee hee hee hee! . . . hee hee hee . . . a-ha ha ha . . . . . hee . . . . hoo . . . . ha ha . . . . ha."

Child of War

I served in the Korean conflict at the age of three, and attended elementary school on the GI Bill. My earliest memory is of the retreat of the First Marines from the Choisin Reservoir through a hellscape of frozen, blasted rock. I ate dog in Korea—a child's portion, of course. Back in the States, first grade seemed like a dream-world to me. There I was, the youngest second lieutenant in the history of American arms, reading about a pair of civilians named Dick and Jane, who knew nothing of lines of fire, or anti-tank warfare, or the terrible things high-speed metal can do to human flesh and bone. I might have been sitting at my desk, but in my mind I was far away, grappling with the tactical problems of the modern battlefield. My teachers had no idea what to make of the drawings of military ordnance which filled the margins in all my workbooks, but the summer after third grade I ran into General Mark Clark, then Army Chief of Staff, at a shopping-center opening near my house. I showed him one of my blueprints—a pro-totype for a midget tank equipped with howitzers, electric missiles, and BB machine guns, which could travel at speeds of seven miles a second. He immediately phoned my parents, and after some discussion, it was agreed that I should transfer to the United States College of Army Guys, located in Olathe, Kansas.

I graduated two years later, with honors in knife-fighting and building forts. I was still a month shy of my ninth birthday. Commissioned a Major, I was sent on my first field assignment—advisor to the Free French forces in North Africa. Through mud and rock and sand we fought our way to the Mediterranean, then landed at Normandy, and at last marched into Paris. It had already been liberated, though, more than a decade previously. I took full responsibility for the error; never again would I disregard the reports of my intelligence staff. From there I was sent to Indochina, where I lived as a foreign exchange student with the Giap family, in a suburb of Hanoi. For a year, General Giap was *An-An* (Daddy) to me. One day, we would meet again, only this time as deadly enemies.

Thanks for the Memory

Two years ago I was driving to Pebble Beach from Palm Springs to play in Bing's pro-amateur tournament at Pebble Beach. I got into my car with Freddie Williams, and we started for Los Angeles. Between Beaumont and Riverside I was pushing it along at about seventy-two. The highway was wide open, nobody in sight, but it was raining a little and I went into a skid.

We turned around, bounced into a ditch, rolled into an orchard and ended up against a tree. Both of us were thrown out. I felt that there was something wrong with my left shoulder, so I stood ankle-deep in mud and practiced my golf swing. The swing wasn't so hot. We left the car and hitch-hiked back to Riverside, and I went to see a doctor. He stretched me out on an X-ray table and took some pictures.

When he'd looked at them, he said, "You're not going to play any golf for eight weeks. You've got a fractured clavicle."

Following that layoff, I went back East, stopping off at the Bob-O'-Link Golf Club in Chicago, where I'm a nonresident member, to have a crack at the course. I got together three friends, Dick Snideman, Dick Gibson and Hugh Davis, and we teed off.

I had a seventy-four for the eighteen holes. It's one of my best scores. The payoff was that on the eighth hole —158 yards—I had a hole in one. You may think that a busted clavicle is a hard way to improve a score, but if you're willing to try it, it could work. It did for me.

—*Have Tux, Will Travel: Bob Hope's Own Story*, by Bob Hope as told to Pete Martin (1954), pp. 225–26

Thanks for the Memory

It was 1950, and I was making the movie *Fancy Pants* with Lucille Ball. Dick Gibson and I had planned to play after the day's shooting had been completed at Paramount. I had one scene left, in which I was riding a horse.

These were close-up shots, so instead of a real horse they used a prop horse, a mechanical gadget. The director wanted more action, so they loosened the straps on the horse and speeded up the action. I was flipped backwards off the horse, head over teakettle. They carried me off the lot in a stretcher, and as they put me into a car, I said, "Right to Lakeside, please." I wound up in Presbyterian Hospital for eight weeks. It was a long time to be away from golf.

The next time I played was at Bob O' Link, a men's club in Chicago. The others in the group were Dick Gibson, Hugh Davis and Dick Sniderman. We had started on the back 9, so by the time we reached the 8th hole, which was our 17th, the bets were rolling. I hit a little faded 5-iron on the hole, which measured 150 yards, and knocked it into the cup for an ace. There is still a plaque on that tee commemorating that feat. I also shot 74 that day, which wasn't bad for a refugee from the hospital.

—*Bob Hope's Confessions of a Hooker: My Lifelong Love Affair with Golf*, by Bob Hope as told to Dwayne Netland (1985), p. 112

People always seem surprised when I tell them that Dan Quayle was the man who introduced Coca-Cola to Asia in 1906. But it's true. I was touring the Far East at the time for Underwood Deviled Ham, in a

group that included Stella Stevens and the late President Ike Eisenhower's father, Dick Snideman. We
stopped to play a little jewel of a course in Burma,
which is what they used to call Ceylon, and there I
met the now Vice-President, who told me of his ac-
complishments for the soft-drink industry and American business in general. He and I were in a foursome
which included Pearl Bailey, the humanitarian Albert
Schweitzer, and the chairman of the American Can
Company (now Primerica), Mr. William Howard Taft.
I had either just been run over by a car or had just
run over someone else in a car. Albert Schweitzer—
who by the way is one of the nicest guys you'd ever
want to meet—and I had a side bet going: dollar a
stroke, quart a hole, winner does the loser's yard. By
the time we reached the seventh, which was our six-
teenth, the bets were rolling pretty good. Pearl Bailey,
who can hit a golf ball farther than any person I've
ever seen, made a perfect little shank shot off a cow
or bull of some kind, directly at the flag, which was
beyond a group of people hired specially for the occasion, which included Dick Gibson from Paramount
and the gals from Air-India publicity. Tee to green,
the distance was 18,000 meters—about 20,000
yards. TV's Ned Beatty, the only man in the American
military to predict the Japanese attack on Pearl Harbor, noticed that I'd broken a spike on my left golf
shoe, and he offered to take me up in his reconnais-
sance helicopter so that I could have better traction
for my swing and wouldn't have to walk so far. We
took off, and when I was above the flag, I lifted a

gentle chip shot, meaning to put enough backspin on
it to stop it just by the hole. Instead I knocked the
ball into the whirling rotorblades, which chopped it
into eighteen little pieces. Somehow, each one of those
little pieces went into a different hole around the
course. I not only had a one on that hole, I had a one
for the whole course! Today there is a plaque on top
of something commemorating this event.

That was 1926. 1927 I worked for the phone company. Ditto 1928. In 1929 came the Crash, and everything changed. I was working as a hoofer for Zwieback
Toast in the old Palace Theatre on Broadway when I
got a call from William Lear, chairman of Lear Jet
Corp.: would I like to come out and make a movie?
Would I! I ran over myself with my car, hopped in,
and drove straight to Hollywood.

In my life I have been blessed with a fabulous
bunch of friends who love the game just as much as
I do, and I put Bill Lear at the very top of that list.
He was just a nice, nice man, and a day doesn't go
by that I don't think of him. Bill met me at the airport
with Dick Sniderman, Freddie Williams, and the people from Cannon Towel, and the next day we started
production on a picture called *The Bear*, by William
Faulkner, starring the wonderful Mexican comedian
Cantinflas, Dorothy Lamour, and yours truly. They
had a great big prop bear which was motorized and
which I was supposed to box with in the climactic
scene. The stunt director, Dick Gibson and Hugh
Davis, wanted more realism, so for the last scene the
Hamm's Breweries people loaned us their real grizzly.

He sure went to town on me. By the time the scene was over, pieces of my scalp and cheekbone were AWOL, and I had a fractured clavicle. Weak with loss of blood, I practiced my golf swing. When I came to, I was hitchhiking to Chicago, where I'm a non-resident member. A doctor there strapped me to a mechanical X-ray table and turned up the juice until I glowed like the marquee at Caesars Palace. Then he slapped me into a men's hospital for eight weeks.

The next time I played was in Bing's Nabisco Pro-Amateur sponsored by Johnson's Wax at a golf course someplace. I was in a foursome that included Lt. Dan Quayle, Pearl Bailey, Dick Sniderman, and what's-his-name, the fat guy. Even though it was frowned on, we had a bet going, a reverse Nassau, where the player with the lowest last number on his card pays the opposite of what everybody else pays him, and by the time we reached the seventh, which was our fourteenth, all the wallets were out. As a gag, the guys from Sperry Rand had substituted an electric golf ball which went right into the cup no matter where you hit it, and I teed up with the thing and it went into the hole and then just kept on going into a lot of other holes around the course, I believe.

•

I make it a point to get out on the links three hundred and sixty-five days a year, no matter what. I don't know anyone else in the entertainment industry who can say the same. I've played in England where it was so foggy that even the seagulls were flying on instruments, and in Africa where it was so hot that.

I was visiting Syria in 1967 as a guest of the Arab-Israeli war with Freddie Williams, Ariel Sharon, Lucille Ball, and University of Texas Longhorns' football coach Darrell Royal, and someone suggested we go play this little course about four miles from the front lines. Well, I'm a sucker for sand—I've been in it most of my golfing life—and that whole region of the world is one big sand trap, if you ask me. So I said sure, and pretty soon we were barrelling along in a converted half-track troop carrier Ariel had found somewhere. I was driving, and the vehicle registration was in a coffee can on the dashboard, and suddenly it rolled off and then out the open front door, and we went into a skid, bounced over Dick Gibson from Paramount, and ended up in a pond. I stove up my neck pretty good.

Lucille Ball, a terrific gal who I loved as if she were a friend, immediately put me in her car and took me to a hospital where they were filming *Fancy Pants*, starring Lucille Ball. They had an X-ray table with straps on it, and the doctor buckled me in and turned up the juice. The thing started bucking and prancing around, and the next I knew it flipped me onto my back like an insect. The doctor took one look at me lying there and said, "You've got a fractured clavicle." Then he stretched me out on an X-ray table for eight weeks. Lucy, God bless her, did not play golf, but she sympathized with my predicament: on the following afternoon I was scheduled to play in the Sam Giancana–Underalls Palm Springs Open. Yet here I

was, half a world away and laid up in a hospital to
boot. Lucy sat down and thought for a while, and then
she came up with a solution that was pure Lucy.

Ten years passed. My Desert Classic Tournament,
excuse me, my *Chrysler* Classic Tournament was
drawing a good crowd and sensational ratings, and
the Timex people had agreed to sponsor me. I was
playing every day, don't forget. I generally teed up
with a Dean Martin's–drinking joke. The guys from
Jimmy Dean Pork Sausage always brought a camera
crew, and I kidded around, pretending like my putter
was a pool cue. This one particular time I sort of
remember happened either in California or someplace
else. I was with people I had played with before or
knew from another context. Dick somebody. We decided to start at the last hole and then play the previous one, and so on. We got all ready, and then we
teed off.

The payoff was over half a billion dollars, just for
me. It's one of the largest amounts of money there is.
To give you some idea, the average professional golfer
votes Republican his entire life for scores which work
out to far less. On top of all that I got the houses, the
cars, the dough from Texaco, and an international
recognition factor that can't be measured in dollars
and cents. You should try it yourself sometime. Bust
a clavicle and lie around a German P.O.W. hospital
for eight weeks and then escape to the West and play
thirty-six holes at Inverness with nothing for breakfast
but a Clark Bar. Fall from a plane, hit a fir tree, bust
a clavicle, and play Winged Foot with some of the

top-ranking daytime stars and the guys from the Village People. Play Pebble Beach: try and hit straight drives in that wind off the Pacific with 5,000 sailors on the U.S.S. *Coral Sea* two miles offshore and a whole lot of water hazard beyond them, while Stella Stevens (as a shapely Wac) saunters by and your buddies hoot and whistle and comment on your club selection. You might do better than you think.

Coyote v. Acme

In the United States District Court,
Southwestern District,
Tempe, Arizona
Case No. B19294,
JUDGE JOAN KUJAVA, PRESIDING

WILE E. COYOTE, PLAINTIFF
—v.—
ACME COMPANY, DEFENDANT

Opening Statement of Mr. Harold Schoff, attorney
for Mr. Coyote: My client, Mr. Wile E. Coyote, a
resident of Arizona and contiguous states, does hereby
bring suit for damages against the Acme Company,
manufacturer and retail distributor of assorted mer-
chandise, incorporated in Delaware and doing business in every state, district, and territory. Mr. Coyote
seeks compensation for personal injuries, loss of business income, and mental suffering caused as a direct
result of the actions and/or gross negligence of said
company, under Title 15 of the United States Code,
Chapter 47, section 2072, subsection (a), relating to
product liability.

Mr. Coyote states that on eighty-five separate
occasions he has purchased of the Acme Company
(hereinafter, "Defendant"), through that company's
mail-order department, certain products which did

Coyote on June 23rd are Plaintiff's Exhibit D. Selected fragments have been shipped to the metallurgical laboratories of the University of California at Santa Barbara for analysis, but to date no explanation has been found for this product's sudden and extreme malfunction. As advertised by Defendant, this product is simplicity itself: two wood-and-metal sandals, each attached to milled-steel springs of high tensile strength and compressed in a tightly coiled position by a cocking device with a lanyard release. Mr. Coyote believed that this product would enable him to pounce upon his prey in the initial moments of the chase, when swift reflexes are at a premium.

To increase the shoes' thrusting power still further, Mr. Coyote affixed them by their bottoms to the side of a large boulder. Adjacent to the boulder was a path which Mr. Coyote's prey was known to frequent. Mr. Coyote put his hind feet in the wood-and-metal sandals and crouched in readiness, his right forepaw holding firmly to the lanyard release. Within a short time Mr. Coyote's prey did indeed appear on the path coming toward him. Unsuspecting, the prey stopped near Mr. Coyote, well within range of the springs at full extension. Mr. Coyote gauged the distance with care and proceeded to pull the lanyard release.

At this point, Defendant's product should have thrust Mr. Coyote forward and away from the boulder. Instead, for reasons yet unknown, the Acme Spring-Powered Shoes thrust the boulder away from Mr. Coyote. As the intended prey looked on unharmed, Mr. Coyote hung suspended in air. Then the twin springs

cause him bodily injury due to defects in manufacture or improper cautionary labelling. Sales slips made out to Mr. Coyote as proof of purchase are at present in the possession of the Court, marked Exhibit A. Such injuries sustained by Mr. Coyote have temporarily restricted his ability to make a living in his profession of predator. Mr. Coyote is self-employed and thus not eligible for Workmen's Compensation.

Mr. Coyote states that on December 13th he received of Defendant via parcel post one Acme Rocket Sled. The intention of Mr. Coyote was to use the Rocket Sled to aid him in pursuit of his prey. Upon receipt of the Rocket Sled Mr. Coyote removed it from its wooden shipping crate and, sighting his prey in the distance, activated the ignition. As Mr. Coyote gripped the handlebars, the Rocket Sled accelerated with such sudden and precipitate force as to stretch Mr. Coyote's forelimbs to a length of fifty feet. Subsequently, the rest of Mr. Coyote's body shot forward with a violent jolt, causing severe strain to his back and neck and placing him unexpectedly astride the Rocket Sled. Disappearing over the horizon at such speed as to leave a diminishing jet trail along its path, the Rocket Sled soon brought Mr. Coyote abreast of his prey. At that moment the animal he was pursuing veered sharply to the right. Mr. Coyote vigorously attempted to follow this maneuver but was unable to, due to poorly designed steering on the Rocket Sled and a faulty or nonexistent braking system. Shortly thereafter, the unchecked progress of the Rocket Sled brought it and Mr. Coyote into collision with the side of a mesa.

Paragraph One of the Report of Attending Physician (Exhibit B), prepared by Dr. Ernest Grosscup, M.D., D.O., details the multiple fractures, contusions, and tissue damage suffered by Mr. Coyote as a result of this collision. Repair of the injuries required a full bandage around the head (excluding the ears), a neck brace, and full or partial casts on all four legs.

Hampered by these injuries, Mr. Coyote was nevertheless obliged to support himself. With this in mind, he purchased of Defendant as an aid to mobility one pair of Acme Rocket Skates. When he attempted to use this product, however, he became involved in an accident remarkably similar to that which occurred with the Rocket Sled. Again, Defendant sold over the counter, without caveat, a product which attached powerful jet engines (in this case, two) to inadequate vehicles, with little or no provision for passenger safety. Encumbered by his heavy casts, Mr. Coyote lost control of the Rocket Skates soon after strapping them on, and collided with a roadside billboard so violently as to leave a hole in the shape of his full silhouette.

Mr. Coyote states that on occasions too numerous to list in this document he has suffered mishaps with explosives purchased of Defendant: the Acme "Little Giant" Firecracker, the Acme Self-Guided Aerial Bomb, etc. (For a full listing, see the Acme Mail Order Explosives Catalogue and attached deposition, entered in evidence as Exhibit C.) Indeed, it is safe to say that not once has an explosive purchased of Defendant by Mr. Coyote performed in an expected manner. To cite just one example: At the expense of

much time and personal effort, Mr. Coyote constructed around the outer rim of a butte a wooden trough beginning at the top of the butte and spiralling downward around it to some few feet above a black X painted on the desert floor. The trough was designed in such a way that a spherical explosive of the type sold by Defendant would roll easily and swiftly down to the point of detonation indicated by the X. Mr. Coyote placed a generous pile of birdseed directly on the X, and then, carrying the spherical Acme Bomb (Catalogue #78-832), climbed to the top of the butte. Mr. Coyote's prey, seeing the birdseed, approached, and Mr. Coyote proceeded to light the fuse. In an instant, the fuse burned down to the stem, causing the bomb to detonate.

In addition to reducing all Mr. Coyote's careful preparations to naught, the premature detonation of Defendant's product resulted in the following disfigurements to Mr. Coyote:

1. Severe singeing of the hair on the head, neck, and muzzle.

2. Sooty discoloration.

3. Fracture of the left ear at the stem, causing the ear to dangle in the aftershock with a creaking noise.

4. Full or partial combustion of whiskers, producing kinking, frazzling, and ashy disintegration.

5. Radical widening of the eyes, due to brow and lid charring.

·

We come now to the Acme Spring-Powered Shoes. The remains of a pair of these purchased by Mr.

recoiled, bringing Mr. Coyote to a violent feet-first collision with the boulder, the full weight of his head and forequarters falling upon his lower extremities.

The force of this impact then caused the springs to rebound, whereupon Mr. Coyote was thrust skyward. A second recoil and collision followed. The boulder, meanwhile, which was roughly ovoid in shape, had begun to bounce down a hillside, the coiling and recoiling of the springs adding to its velocity. At each bounce, Mr. Coyote came into contact with the boulder, or the boulder came into contact with Mr. Coyote, or both came into contact with the ground. As the grade was a long one, this process continued for some time.

The sequence of collisions resulted in systemic physical damage to Mr. Coyote, viz., flattening of the cranium, sideways displacement of the tongue, reduction of length of legs and upper body, and compression of vertebrae from base of tail to head. Repetition of blows along a vertical axis produced a series of regular horizontal folds in Mr. Coyote's body tissues—a rare and painful condition which caused Mr. Coyote to expand upward and contract downward alternately as he walked, and to emit an off-key accordionlike wheezing with every step. The distracting and embarrassing nature of this symptom has been a major impediment to Mr. Coyote's pursuit of a normal social life.

As the Court is no doubt aware, Defendant has a virtual monopoly of manufacture and sale of goods required by Mr. Coyote's work. It is our contention that Defendant has used its market advantage to the detriment of the consumer of such specialized products as itching powder, giant kites, Burmese tiger traps, anvils, and two-hundred-foot-long rubber bands. Much as he has come to mistrust Defendant's products, Mr. Coyote has no other domestic source of supply to which to turn. One can only wonder what our trading partners in Western Europe and Japan would make of such a situation, where a giant company is allowed to victimize the consumer in the most reckless and wrongful manner over and over again.

Mr. Coyote respectfully requests that the Court regard these larger economic implications and assess punitive damages in the amount of seventeen million dollars. In addition, Mr. Coyote seeks actual damages (missed meals, medical expenses, days lost from professional occupation) of one million dollars; general damages (mental suffering, injury to reputation) of twenty million dollars; and attorney's fees of seven hundred and fifty thousand dollars. Total damages: thirty-eight million seven hundred and fifty thousand dollars. By awarding Mr. Coyote the full amount, this Court will censure Defendant, its directors, officers, shareholders, successors, and assigns, in the only language they understand, and reaffirm the right of the individual predator to equal protection under the law.

In the Plain Air

While Manet painted the Monet family, Renoir painted beside him and Monet worked nearby. Monet painted Renoir at his easel (present location unknown), while Renoir, like Manet, painted Madame Monet, Jean Monet, and the rooster (National Gallery of Art, Washington, D.C.). Monet later recalled that as Renoir painted, Manet glanced at his canvas from time to time, and at one point the older artist walked over to Monet and whispered: "He has no talent at all that boy! You, who are his friend, tell him please to give up painting."

—Label to *The Monet Family in Their Garden*, by Édouard Manet, in the Metropolitan Museum

A suburban summer afternoon at Argenteuil. A garden: willows, hyacinths, a privet hedge. Beyond the hedge, walls of the bicycle works, twin smokestacks with plumes of smoke blowing at identical angles. To the south, a field filled with haystacks, probably left over from last year, and to the west, past the lane, a hillside sloping gently to the sea.

MANET, MONET, *and* RENOIR *are setting up easels, uncapping and sniffing tubes of paint, flicking brushes across their thumbs, etc.*

MADAME MONET *fusses with young* JEAN, *arranging his collar. He squirms.*

The ROOSTER *struts nervously nearby.*

RENOIR: Now, allow me to understand. Monsieur Manet paints Monsieur Monet—

MONET: After painting first Madame Monet, my wife.

REN.: Ah, yes, your wife, and also your charming infant—

MANET: And the rooster.

MON.: That goes without saying.

REN.: And, Claude, you paint me—

MON.: If you have no objections.

REN.: Certainly not. You wish to paint me at my easel?

MON.: Of course.

REN.: Who, then, should I paint?

MONET *and* RENOIR *look at each other. Then both turn to look at* MANET.

MAN.: Absolutely not! I forbid it!

MON.: Please, Édouard, it only seems fair.

REN.: Oh, but the symmetry—you paint the Monets, Claude paints me, I paint you—perfect!

MAN.: Nobody paints Manet. (*He hunches over his canvas and begins to sketch in some outlines.*)

REN.: But, but—

MAN.: You may paint Madame and the child, as I am doing.

RENOIR *looks at* MONET. MONET *shrugs.*

REN.: Very well. Monsieur Manet paints Madame and the child, who have no objection to the procedure, and Monsieur Monet paints me, who am similarly inclined, while I, in turn, following the lead of the distinguished Monsieur Manet, paint, to the best of my ability, a second, though one hopes not inferior, portrait of the family Monet.

MAN. (*without looking up*): Shall we begin?

RENOIR *places his easel and stool a few feet from* MANET, *facing* MADAME MONET *and* JEAN. MONET *moves his easel where he can see* RENOIR. *They begin to paint.*

Humming tunelessly, RENOIR *selects a brush and makes a few passes at his canvas. Still humming, he sights along his thumb at* MADAME MONET. *Then, slowly, he moves his thumb until he is sighting at* MANET.

MAN.: What are you doing? I made it clear that you are not to depict me in any way.

REN.: Sorry, sorry.

They continue in silence. The ROOSTER *pecks at a grasshopper; it jumps away from him. He chases it; it jumps away again. He catches it and throws it in the air with his beak.*

REN. (*to* MAN.): Did you see? Remarkable!

MANET *snorts derisively.*

MON.: Auguste, could you turn this way just a bit? . . . Just a bit more, if you don't mind. A bit more. . . . Good! Just like that. Look like you're painting.

REN.: That is what I am trying to do, if you will allow me.

MON.: Just another moment. Good. Now you may relax.

MME. MON.: There is cider, if anyone should wish.

MAN.: No. Please hold your pose.

REN.: I have a tremendous thirst, myself. I have been perspiring like a swine.

MAN.: But we have been sitting here for less than a quarter of an hour.

MON.: We shall have the cider a little later, my dearest.

REN. (*under his breath*): Sheesh! (MANET *works intently, peering around his canvas and then painting with his brush held close to his face.* RENOIR *makes a few dabs at his canvas, then leans back on his stool to view the result.*) Ah, yes. (*He makes another few dabs, leans back again.*) Ah, *yes!* Just so! (*Another few dabs.*) Oh-h-h-h-h, *yes!* That's it. That is IT! (*Another few dabs.*) Oh, now you are working. Yes! Now you are cooking! (*Another few dabs. Chuckling softly.*) Oh, yes! Very good! *Ver-y* good in-*deed!*

MAN.: WILL YOU PLEASE BE QUIET!

REN. (*startled, smudging his canvas*): Aaah! Now look what you made me do. Her eyebrow is like a giant sun.

MAN.: That is no concern of mine.

REN.: This will take forever to put right.

MAN.: You should have thought of that before.

REN.: I was minding my business.

The minutes pass. The leaves of the trees grow heavy with the torpor of midsummer. Several times, young JEAN *must be restrained by his mother from getting up and running away. We hear his plaintive "Maman."* RENOIR *sketches in a detail with a small brush, pauses, then scrapes it out with his palette knife.*

MON.: I heard an amusing story about van Gogh

the other day. (RENOIR *sketches the detail again, shakes his head, again scratches it out.*) It seems van Gogh was walking down the street in Arles (RENOIR *scrapes at his canvas again with an exclamation of impatience*) and you know how van Gogh looks with that hat he always wears— (RENOIR *scratches his head, furrows his brow, and tries the detail again.* MANET, *meanwhile, steals a quick glance at* RE-NOIR'S *canvas, then another one. Then he stares openly for a moment or two. Then he gets up from his stool and looks closer until he is leaning over* RENOIR's *shoulder.*) So anyway (*laughing*), just as van Gogh was passing the bakery a Swedish man comes up to him—

REN. (*suddenly seeing* MANET *behind him*): Chouf! Spread out!

MAN.: That's not the way a chicken's feet go.

REN.: Oh, really? Well, I am of the opinion that it is.

MAN.: Excuse me, but I can assure you that it is not.

REN. (*rising, with fists clenched*): Why, for two francs I'd—

MAN.: You'd what?

MON.: Édouard, Auguste, please! Calm yourselves!

RENOIR *and* MANET *stand nose to nose for a few seconds. Then, slowly, they back off.* RENOIR *turns away from* MANET *with dignity, sits down, resumes painting.* MANET *walks over to* MONET.

MON.: So, anyway, to return to my story about van

Gogh—the Swedish man, noticing van Gogh's hat, remarks (*unintelligible Swedish accent*)—

MAN. (*whispering, gesturing behind his hand at* RENOIR): He has no talent at all that boy! You, who are his friend, tell him please to give up painting.

REN. (*leaps to his feet*): I heard that!

RENOIR *spits in his palms, scrapes his feet on the ground, and rushes at* MANET.

BLACKOUT. *Sounds of a scuffle. The* ROOSTER *squawks frantically.*

·

The lights come up to reveal the three painters once again at their easels. MANET *holds a large beefsteak over one eye.* RENOIR *has an ice bag on his right hand, and is painting with difficulty with his left.* MONET's *coat is in tatters.*

MADAME MONET *and* JEAN *are seated in the same pose as before.*

MAN.: I am sure I will have a shiner.

REN.: My hand is throbbing as if I had hit a marble column.

MAN.: You may expect to receive my doctor's bill.

REN.: And you may count upon a call from my attorney.

MAN.: I see that you paint just as skillfully with this hand as you did with the other.

REN.: Your antipathy is like a tonic to me.

MAN.: Take my advice, you are wasting your time.

REN.: The public will revere my name long after it has given up trying to tell which is you and which is Claude.

MAN.: Your name will not outlive you by one second.

MON.: And which of *you*, may I ask, plans to pay my tailor's bill, or for the damage to my hedge?

A silence, unbroken except for the faint scratching of the brushes.

TABLEAU.

·

MONET *comes forward and addresses the audience.*

MON.: This, then, was Impressionism. What delight when the works identified with that name first began appearing everywhere in the galleries and salons, like a limpid tide overflowing the crumbling levees of the past! But behind the surface of the pictures—what malice, what bile, what violence! Did the admirers who stood rapt before these works suspect that the hands that held the brushes could also hit, pinch, slap, tweak, and give stinging nose-flappers?

Perhaps you wonder what became of the pictures we made that day in the garden as the summer sun beat down. Renoir's painting, when completed, was purchased I believe by a woman named Marjorie, who later sold it directly or indirectly to the government of the United States, in order to raise money for some things she wanted to buy, evidently. Manet's painting, also, was bought and sold one or more times until it, too, ended up at a location overseas. And as for my painting—well, so moved was I by the events of that afternoon, I decided I must change my picture completely. I took the portrait I had been working on and glued additional canvas to it until it was twelve times as large, and stretched it on a new frame. I then included the struggle between the two painters, and a sequence-drawing of the holds they used, and an effect of the droplets of sweat flying in the air, and the terrified eyes of my family, and myself as participant and observer—all overhung by the dust of our exertions in shafts of late-afternoon light. When I had finished, I believed this was a work which would change forever the history of painting; but, unfortunately, it later became lost somewhere.

BLACKOUT. CURTAIN.

Ask Sherman Strong

Every week Sherman Strong, millionaire, replies to readers' financial requests. You may write to him care of a newspaper, Department of the Treasury, Rockville, Md. 20850.

Dear Sherman Strong,

I'm a cheap, cheese-ball chiseller too lazy to pay my own freight. But why should I bust my hump when there's rich saps like *you*, Sherman Strong, just waitin' to hand over some of that long green to *me*? Ha-ha! Very good, Mr. Sherman Strong—you do the work, I get the cash. That's an arrangement the way I like it! You bet I'll take your money, as much as you can give for as long as you can shell it out. What for? That's my lookout. I'll feather my bed with it, Mr. Sherman Strong, and tell the world what a prize sucker I found in you. And when the dough runs out, instead of getting a job I'll come right back to you with my sack in my hand. Fill it up, Sherman Strong, and keep it coming. Money-

money-money-money-money! Fat cats like you were just made for fellows like me.

> R.G., Lake Forest, Ill.

Dear R.G.,

You are right about one thing—I do have money. How much, exactly? Truthfully, I couldn't tell you an exact dollar amount: tens of thousands, hundreds of thousands, possibly even a million dollars (depending on the stock market, and the repayment on a few loans owed to me). Enough to keep an accountant busy for several days, let me assure you.

Yes, I could give you as much as three or four hundred dollars with a simple stroke of the pen, and never feel it at all. Even a sum as large as four hundred and fifty dollars, while great to you, would hardly be missed by me. But I'm not going to do that, Mr. R.G. You see money simply as a commodity. To me, money stands for hope, and dreams, and progress, and ordinary people all over the world helping other people who have it already to do the things they enjoy. But that is something I'm afraid you'll never understand.

Dear Sherman Strong,

So—the brush-off, eh? Not so fast, *Mister* Strong. Chintzy little pointy-toothed advantage-taking ratty guys of my sort don't give up so easy. No way, no day. As you know, if I put half the effort into honest work that I do into cadging and fi-

nagling and stiffing people, I'd be richer than you.
So here I am, comin' back atcha: you got, I want.
Gimmee!

R.G., Lake Forest, Ill.

[No answer. File.—S.S.]

Dear Sherman Strong,
My wife fell down and broke her hip last week.
But that's not why I'm writing you. I'm writing you
. . . oh, just to write you. I read your column every
week. I love the way you're smiling, in your picture, that is. It makes me think you're nice. I want
to tell you that I've read your column every time
I've seen it. My problem is this.

Mrs. A.R.,
Egg Harbor City, N.J.

Dear Mrs. A.R.,
Now you're talking, and I read you loud and
clear. By the time you see this, a check in your
initials may be already on its way to the charity of
your choice, either from me or someone else. A
gesture such as yours, taking a moment to do what
you did—that's what sharing is all about. God
bless!

Hey! Sherman Strong!
What's the hangup there, Sherman? I go to my
mailbox, I got a lot of no-answer from you. Some-

body put a crimp in your cash flow? Listen, there's
no hurry. I got all the time in the world. I'm just
sitting here on my duff, mooching off very close
personal friends of mine, you know the kind I
mean, the kind I want *you* to be. Hey, I'll try anything, just so long as I don't accidentally do anything for anybody else. Get that money moving my
way, the sooner the better. I have some cheesy,
ratty discretionary purchases I want to make. Pay
up, bub.

R.G., Lake Forest, Ill.

[File.—S.S.]

Dear Sherman Strong,
    I am not a welfare fraud, and I don't cheat on my
taxes, dip into the till at work, or sign time sheets
for hours I haven't put in. I don't hide people in
the trunk of my car when I go to a drive-in movie,
or "sample" items in a grocery store unless I intend
to pay for them. Unlike many others in our society,
I don't rent furnished apartments and then sell
the contents to any of a number of used-furniture
dealers found in the yellow pages. It just goes
against my grain. I don't file false insurance
claims, no matter how hard they would be to check,
and if money is paid to me in error, I return it.
I don't take things that don't belong to me, I have
never once been the recipient of an illegal payment or donation, and I would never ask for or

accept charity from you or anyone else. Give me
$2,500.

George Abshire,
Sidney, Nebraska

Dear Mr. Abshire,

I wonder if you have any idea how much money
twenty-five hundred dollars actually is. Perhaps you
will understand more clearly if I put it this way:
what you are asking for is two *thousand* five
hundred dollars, or, to put it in layman's terms,
nearly three *thousand* dollars. Even at my level of
affluence, it is a sum I see only very rarely. The
sheer bulk of that much cash is something of which
the average person has no grasp. Imagine, if you
can, a hundred-dollar bill; then imagine twenty-five
of them, one on top of another. That stack would
fill a standard business envelope to the thickness of
one-eighth of an inch, and all solid hundreds.

However, because of your many fine qualities, I
believe you are entitled to a reward. Take this column and show it to the bartender at your local
watering hole; then tell him to give you a drink, on
the house!

Dear, dear Sherman Strong,

Inasmuch as I am a dedicated sort of leech, and
inasmuch as I love nothing better than a fat, dumb,
and happy meal ticket such as yourself, I am
hereby writing once again for a nice big wad of free
money. Proceeding forthwith and henceforth, you

will direct your agents, Messrs. Chump & Chump,
Inc., to advance to my account via bonded cash
courier a sizable payment, the first of many to follow on a schedule to be determined by me. Meanwhile, I'll just lay back with my feet up on the
cocktail table smoking a borrowed cigar and let
John-down-the-road handle my responsibilities as a
human being—gratis, of course.

Hey, don't get me wrong. It's not that I really
need the dough. But only a schmo would miss out
on a gravy train like you. So, how about a cool fifty
grand, for starters? Make that sixty.

As ever,
R.G., Lake Forest, Ill.

[Don't file. Discard.—S.S.]

Dear Mr. Strong,

Several months ago I wrote to you asking for
funds to pay for a much-needed vacation from cleri-
cal duties, a trip to Disney's Epcot Center, in Florida. As the days went by with no response, I had
just about given up hope. Then last Friday I looked
in my mailbox and found an official-looking envelope containing a tax-refund check from the federal
government made out in my name with no strings
attached! I simply cannot tell you how happy you
have made me. The amount was enough to cover
transportation, meals, a four-day hotel stay, and ex-

tras besides. You are a prince, Mr. Strong. If only there were more like you.

Rev. Michael Pattison
Clearwater, Fla. 34625

Dear Rev. Pattison,

Helping a person at no cost is one of the greatest satisfactions this little column of mine can provide. The knowledge that I could have sent you a check myself had I chosen to reminds me of how fortunate I have been. So why shouldn't I share some of that good fortune with my fellowman, in principle? I don't suggest notions like that merely in the hopes of receiving a reward in Heaven—but I bet a good word from you wouldn't hurt. Have a ball, and don't mention it!

Dear Sherman Strong,

Pursuant to my missive of the 21st inst., I once again take pen in hand to request bucks by the carload from you, Mr.

[Discard.—S.S.]

Dear Sherm,

Having decided at this juncture that it would be advantageous for me to acquire a bunch of stuff that I want but can't pay for,

[Discard.]

My good friend, Sherman,
As down payment toward the purchase of a
snazzy new sports sedan with privacy glass, I'll be
needing

[Discard.]

Dear "Got-Rocks" Strong,
In order that I may continue to coast down easy
street, what say you give me

[Discard.]

Dear Sherman,
Please remit all surplus scratch A.S.A.P. to

[Discard.]

Dear Readers:
Sometimes, at the end of the column, I like to
take a moment just to chat with you. You know, I
receive three thousand to five thousand letters a
week from you, and the vast majority of them are
fine. You're good, generous people, living hand to
mouth—I salute you. I know what it is to have to
work for a living, because I've seen people doing it;
I'm sure we all have. I don't resent your pleas for
money. I give my full attention to each and every
one, and then judge solely on the merits. Sherman
Junior and daughter Carol and I sit in the afternoons in the office part of the house with mail just

heaped around our feet. When a letter strikes us as particularly new in approach, we sometimes read it aloud. Every so often, one or more will really get to me. You may think that other rich people and I are very different from you. Well, we are and we aren't. I'd like to explain what I mean with a little story.

Thirty years ago I was a young patent attorney.

Well, a lot has changed since then. Look around you. On every corner, individuals who think the world owes them a living. Check-bouncers, bill-dodgers, fare-jumpers, payment-skippers—the world owes them exactly what they deserve, which is precious little. Fortunately, ours is a system devised long ago by men far wiser than ourselves, which insures to those who possess wealth the power to keep it, and to those who don't good wishes for the best of luck. You see, money, in and of itself, is important; but what is even more important is obtaining other money in addition. And far, far beyond either of these is the rich inner satisfaction. Supposedly, it is a feeling which no amount of money can buy.

The Afternoon of

June 8, 1991

Those who adopt satanism come from all walks of life.
. . . They include doctors, lawyers, professors, university presidents.

—*Insight* magazine

Hello and welcome—is this on?—hello and welcome to the ssbt sbt zzzzbt alumni and friends of Brainard *bzzzt* Brainard University, zzzbt and to all the wheeee ZZZZZZZZ families of the class of '91. And to all of you new graduates zzzzZZZZZ ZAAA ZAAA AZAZEL AZAZEL ZZZzzzzzb sitting down front in your elegant black caps and gowns, let me add— you made it! Ssssbt zzzzbt zzzeee b'zeee b'zeee zzzZA-MIEL this rain holds off awhile so we don't have to move the ceremony into the gym. *Wheeeeee Moloch, Moloch, serve him* a special welcome to all the faculty emeriti—it's good to have you back—nnnnnNERGAL BELIAL LAL-LAL-LAL also to the fiftieth anniversary class of '41. Your special reunion drive raised enough non-earmarked zzzzzzzZZZZ sssssss SSSSSSAMMAEL SCRATCH SCRATCH funds for us to add some badly needed phet phet phet TOPHET phet phet to our physical plant. Many thanks from the entire Brainard University family.

-ily-ly-ly-ly eeeeeeee rely here at Brainard on the generosity of individual and corporate contributors ssssssSERPENT AHRIMANESsssss THAMUZzzzzzzz offset an alarming thirty-two-per-cent increase in costs *bbbbbbbeeeelzebubbbbbb* unfortunately, a projected shortfall of almost three million dollars. Your loyal support, which has had an enormous impact on our success, bab bab bab BAB BAB ABADDON enhance the quality of the learning experience at Brainard. Wheeeeeee wheeee eeeeee Old Nick Nick Nick a sombre note on this festive occasion, but in the face of unrelenting financial pressures bbbbbbbheeeee beasthood beasthood before the end of the fiscal year on June 30th.

Now for the good news. rrrrr RRRRRRROOOOO-AAAAARRRRRRrrrr HOW-OW-OW-WOW-WOW-WOW-rrrrrr rrrrrOW rrrrrrrrOW rrrrRAHAB RAHAB BAB BAB BAAL BAALIM BAALBERITH rrrrRRROARRR-rrrr awarded summa cum laude. OW OW OW POWERS-OF-THE-AIR magna cum laude, and nearly two hundred receiving the lesser but still very commendable degree of cum laude. In addition, we point with pride to the impressive number of graduates who will be receiving stipendiary hummm hummm hummmMMMMMMMMMMMELCHOM RIMMON ASMODEUS APOLLYON CHEMOSH, ROBHES-THE-DOOR-DEMONNNNNNNNNNNNNN nearly half again as many as any university in the area. Again, ooooooooo eeeeeeeeee *Shedim Ahriman Euronymous*

Erl-King swarming, swarming, many prestigious scholars in our tenured and non-tenured faculty.

[Takes drink of water.]

Bzip bzeeeeeeeeeee bzeeeeeeeeeeee *Beassssssst-Massssssster Beassssst-Massssssster* generous bequest of Mr. and Mrs. Harry E. WAAAAAHHHHEEE MAW-WORM expansion of our media center and film department, construction to begin this hhhhhhhhhh-hhhhhh. The reHHHOOOOOOOVESsss zzzzzzzzz, a matching grant from our friends at Electric Boat. Let's give them a round of rrreeeee-rrrrreeeee-reeee *eee-EEEEEE* EREBUS RHADAMANTHUS PRINCE-OF-DARKNESS HORNED-ONE UHN UHN UHN nnnnnn round of applause. We couldn't do it without you.

[Bubbling hellmouth opens in earth in front of podium, then closes.]

As I'm sure we all know only too well, the price of a college education HORROR THE HORROR-ROR-ROR-ROR over the last twenty years zzzz b'zzzzzzzzz b'zzzzzzzzz regrettable b'zzzzzzz *Pazuzu-Prince-of-Locustsssss,* and will for the foreseeable future. Student tuitions actually cover only The-Insect-Inside-You-That-Wants-To-LIVE! which amounts to less than two-fifths of the actual sbt sbeeeee sbeee Baron SAMEDI-eeeeeeeee of every diploma awarded today. And of that two-fifths

[Deafening crack, as lightning hits overhead. Smell of sulfur.]

in long-term, interest-deferred federal tuition loans. Given the critical nature of the need, we have begun two highly lauded funding outreach programs. I wish I had more answers during this difficult ffffffffffff Mephisto fffffffft ft pht Astaroth pht ffffff

[*Whirlwind touches down in center aisle. Sparks from p.a. system.*]

introduce our commencement speaker, Dr. Howard Hall. Born in Springfield, Dr. Hall made his first dollar as a child of six, when he convinced a playmate to purchase a toy he had made. After attending the public schools he matriculated at Brainard where

[*Is skewered to floor by religious symbol falling from steeple of school chapel nearby. Prizes self loose, gets up.*]

and went on to earn his Master's at CH-CH-CH-CHORONZON BLACK-RIDER and soon BEHEMOTH BELPHEGOR president of his own SEMJAZA BERALD BARALAMENSIS ADRAMMELECH-eck-eck private listings to realtors. BAL-BAL-BALDACHIENSIS PAU-MACHIE APOLOROSEDES unaffected by the Crash, luckily, ITEMON GENIO LUCIFUGE NAAMAHHHHHH after whom Hall Quadrangle is named. Please join me in giving him a nice

[*Explodes into smoke.*]

Have You Ever

To our valued policyholders:

As the nation's only insurer providing basic health and liability coverage to single, married, and dependent characters in daytime television dramas, First Mutual Protagonist Life & Health is proud of its thirty-five years of service to this exciting community. At First Mutual, we understand the need of invented individuals for a variety of insurance products not offered by other carriers.

Recently, however, due to national economic factors, First Mutual has shared in an industry-wide downturn which threatens the high standard of performance we have always maintained. As a result, we are forced to reassess our present rate scales. Please fill out, sign, and return the appended questionnaire at your earliest convenience in order that we may find the new payment schedule right for you. Failure to do so may result in refund of balance remaining (if any) and full cancellation of your policy within sixty real-time calendar days.

I. PERSONAL HEALTH

(To be completed by all respondents)

Have you ever

1. suffered from amnesia?
2. taken a paternity test?
3. been declared legally dead?
4. undergone reconstructive surgery that changed facial features, height, weight, and/or hair color? (If any *yes* to *4*, was condition accompanied by alteration of voice due to damage to laryngeal nerve?)
5. Have you ever had
   hysterical pregnancy
   temporary blindness
   six-week brain tumor
   post-hypnotic trauma
   fatal nerve disease
   paralysis from waist down
   ☐ pre-engagement
   ☐ post-engagement
   fainting spells
   catatonia
   supposed infertility
   character dysfunction
6. Did you ever emerge from a coma as Tab Hunter?
7. Are you subject to multiple personality or other disorder requiring medication?
8. Have you ever been hospitalized for substance abuse, delusions, or flashback?
9. Have you ever: ☐ married ☐ divorced ☐ remarried ☐ discovered former spouse had got-

ten pregnant by/impregnated you before divorce ☐ saw new baby ☐ wanted to be part of his/her life ☐ learned new baby had fatal illness ☐ slept with former spouse in order to conceive child in order to harvest its bone marrow in order to save life of child No. 1 ☐ harvested bone marrow from child No. 2 ☐ saved life of child No. 1 ☐ destroyed second marriage ☐ divorced ☐ remarried (previous) former spouse ☐ left town?

10. If any *yes* to 9, attach blood test and/or billing records.

11. Have you ever secretly photographed any individual and built a shrine to him/her in your room, house, or place of residence?

II. ACTUARIAL

All respondents please note that federal law prohibits refusal of coverage for any criterion not specifically outlined in section five of the licensing charter. However, because of statistically higher rates of implausible disappearance for nonwhite protagonists, First Mutual reserves the right to take into account previous storyline in the event of any such character's revival or unlikely return.

1. Are you a mercenary or former mercenary?

2. Are you a former mercenary turned Buddhist monk, police detective, or related occupation?

3. Have you ever been in a crash?
   ☐ regular
   ☐ fiery

4. Have you visited or resided in any of the following
   countries during the last eighteen months?
   Rio Blanco
   San Cristobal
   Puerto Grande
   Monte Dinero
   Suraban
   Costa Maria
   Santo Stephanico
   Los Rios
5. If any *yes* to 4, state purpose of visit or residence:
   ☐ stage own kidnapping
   ☐ other (explain)
6. Do you own a motorcycle, powerboat (150 hp and
   over), or purebred stallion/s?
7. (Respondents with $10,000,000/yr. personal in-
   come only)
   Is private jet equipped with fire extinguisher,
   smoke detector, and cabin-door latch inhibitor?
   Do grounds of estate include one or more pits,
   tunnels, mines, crypts, or permanently sealed
   rooms?
   Is boathouse, bathhouse, gatehouse, or other important outbuilding lit by high-intensity mercury
   lamps of wattage totalling at least 5000?
   Does staircase landing adjoin route of access for
   health-care personnel?
   Are gifts and floral displays at wedding reception
   or similar event subjected to screening by metal
   detector, X-ray, or thermal neutron analysis
   device?
   Is patio, swim area, and/or moat fenced?

8. (Respondents under $10,000,000/yr. personal income)

Are you a step-grandniece/nephew?

To the best of your knowledge and belief, do you have any undeclared blood relatives in your town, hospital, place of business, adjacent communities, or other location?

Do you possess valid driver's or chauffeur's license?

Does place of employment have office in Tokyo?

9. (Twins only)

Hair

☐ not fluffy ☐ fluffy

Shirt collar

☐ both tabs inside sweater

☐ one tab out of sweater

Personality

☐ twisted   ☐ outgoing

10. (M.D.s, psychiatrists, psychologists, administrators, and physical therapists only)

Are you ☐ married ☐ single

Is spouse (if any) an electronics heir/heiress, mercenary or former mercenary, police detective, Buddhist monk, or related occupation?

Have you ever knowingly or unknowingly performed a medical procedure?

Have you recently been the recipient of any testimonial banquets, luncheons, awards, or surprise parties?

11. (Hookers and former hookers please see additional questionnaire sheets mailed under separate cover.)

12. (All respondents)
    Please state any and all previously existing con-
    ditions which may cause you to turn into some-
    body, or vice versa.

III. GENERAL
    1. Are you now or have you ever been a general?
    2. If *yes*, in which country (see above, section
    II-4)?

.

This is not a bill. Please do not include payment. If
application is accepted, you will be informed by mail,
at which time a new contract will be issued to you.
All information contained in application will be
treated confidentially by employees and assigns of
insurer. When required, confidential information may
also be supplied to its affiliates, reinsurers, contrac-
tors, and other interested parties, not exclusive of
secret sworn enemies who have hated or feared applicant from childhood. Insurer declares itself not
liable in cases of data theft, file removal, or unspec-
ified acts of malice. Information will not otherwise be
disclosed except as required by plot or supermarket
tabloid.

Linton's Whatnots

Sunset. The moors. A strong gale blowing.

CATHY: Oh, hold me, Heathcliff. Only in your arms am I truly happy. When Edgar Linton holds me I feel so cold.

HEATHCLIFF: Your husband can never love you, Cathy. He will never see how cruel and fine and free you are.

CATHY: Edgar Linton's spirit is to mine as a small bedchamber washbasin to a great, deep millpond. The difference between us makes me tremble! Also, there's his . . . his collection of novelty nutcrackers.

HEATHCLIFF: Linton, a collector? (*Wild, anguished laugh*) I should have expected it.

CATHY: He keeps them somewhere. In the tool cellar, I believe.

HEATHCLIFF: Ha! And I suppose they are all hand-carved.

CATHY: I believe so. You will have to ask him.

HEATHCLIFF: And hand-painted.

CATHY: Possibly. I hardly listen when he speaks of them.

HEATHCLIFF: From Tahiti, no doubt, and Guinea, and of sandalwood from the Leeward Islands.

CATHY: Again, I would not know. He has such a very great many.

HEATHCLIFF: I would think nothing of holding you this way even in the presence of Linton himself and all his damned novelty items!

(*They kiss.*)

•

"Hello, I'm Edgar Linton. Most of you know of the marital difficulties between my wife and myself. Others—more than a few, I hope—may recognize my name from certain monographs published in *The Cotswolds Hobbyist* and elsewhere. Catherine, bless her (for I love her still, despite everything), never understood my nutcrackers. I do not begrudge her that, nor that she called my life's hobby 'tedious'! To her, of course, it was. To me, it was a joy shot through with bright threads of exotica and adventure, mine to pursue in my own home through the wonders of parcel post.

"I did not, and do not, keep them in any 'tool cellar.' I don't know where she got that. The bulk of my collection is stored in a converted tack room below the conservatory, suitably cool and dry, fitted on three sides with sliding shelves in mahogany cases. To oversimplify rather drastically, all nutcrackers can be divided into two categories: those made of wood, and those made of other materials, such as stone, metal, or ivory. The larger number by far are of wood, hardwoods such as teak and walnut being preferred, inasmuch as you cannot crack a nut with soft woods like cypress or pine. Swelling and warping cause wooden parts—screw or lever mechanisms, often artfully, artfully carved—to jam. For this reason, low-moisture storage rooms are required.

"Now, as to the objects themselves. This one here is a favorite. You simply grasp the ankles like so, insert any nut you like (except perhaps a Brazil nut), and— You see? Rather neat. Or, again, you have this model, in which you grasp the back part, here, and the front part, here, insert the nut, turn in opposite directions, and crack. Seen from a distance, both of these make quite striking statuettes, if you prop them against something to keep them from falling over. This next one, as you see, is jointed at both the knees and middle, so that it can accommodate two or more nuts and shatter all at a go when you press upon the topknot.

"Here is one that Catherine particularly disliked. Something about the accuracy of the detail, I suppose, or the expression of the features. I was disappointed, of course, but I had grown used to her reactions. She set her jaw and turned away, forgetting for the moment to disguise that slight double chin I so adored. I knew she was only tolerating me, that every moment she spent viewing my collection her thoughts were with him to whom she was longing to fly. Really, she never gave the nutcrackers much of a show. The cleverness of this one's hinge, the way it duplicates an anatomical part, was lost on her. (What is even more saddening is that I am absolutely positive she would have loved this or any of the others if only she'd relaxed a bit.) She stood and listened for as long as she could bear, then muttered an excuse and hurried upstairs. Soon I heard from the room above me the faint sounds of her departure. I could imagine the passion of their meeting, her caresses more intense for the tiresome half hour I had made her endure. I filled the lamp with coal oil, the costlier, smokeless kind, and prepared for an evening of cataloguing.

"During these troubles I continued to be grateful for the kind solace and understanding of Dr. and Mrs. Hiram Ennis, of Philadelphia, U.S.A. Fellow-collectors will remember the Ennises well, although they are unknown to wider fame. Hiram and Marguerite, your devotion reminds me that the friends one makes collecting nutcrackers are friends indeed. Further, I would like to thank nutcracker fanciers Mr. Ulrich Link, of Ulm, Germany; Mr. Philip Clausing, of Austria; Mme. Berthe Olivet and her son Bertrand, of Paris; the Misses Buckingham, of Devon; and Mr. Frank McEachern, of the American firm of McEachern Nuts & Savories, Inc. Faithful friends, all! You must have known, or suspected, what was going on between Catherine and me and—him. I deeply appreciate the tact which kept all reference to my situation out of our newsletter."

.

Dr. and Mrs. Ennis were on a collecting tour of the Southwest, and could not be reached. Mr. Frank

McEachern submitted the following, on stationery with the company letterhead:

"Ed Linton has the best collection of nutcrackers in the world. In fact, it is so far superior nothing else comes close. His holdings in Modern Calisthenics pieces alone are better than most museums'. I have offered Ed prices five times list and more for 'crackers to add to our collection here at our main office, but he always refuses. He loves his hobby too much to profit from it. In a sense, Ed *is* nutcracker collecting. I've never met the wife. Of course, I don't know this other fellow she was mixed up with, but I can assure you that Ed's worth a hundred of him, whoever he is. Once—I couldn't help myself—I even wrote Mrs. Linton a letter and said so, in the plainest terms."

Mrs. Edgar Linton
Thrushcross Grange, etc.
England
Personal and Confidential

Dear Mrs. Linton,

   Although I feel it is hardly my place, under the circumstances, to speak of such things as pertain to intimacies between a husband and wife, and although I do not know you at all well—indeed, have never met you—yet I feel more than compelled to write to you, not, as I say, without certain doubts and reservations. Your husband is a fine man. Do you think you might use your influence to persuade him to part with a few of his nutcrackers, namely, the ones that look like ladies in gymnastic costume?

·

Cathy replied by return post.
"I informed Mr. McEachern that if he ever attempted to write to me again, I would alert officials of the Board of Customs. Edgar, the coward! That he should waste his youth, and mine, corresponding with these types— Oh, Heathcliff, if you only knew how I suffered! But you were gone, and I was left for long, empty days with him and his whatnots. How I hated them, except for the ones—oh, you know, the ones with the little huntsman. I am sure you recall them. I asked Edgar if I could set them on the spinet. With the little huntsman with the musket? A sort of spring device catapulted the nut from the musket into the hole in the hollow tree, where there was a movable squirrel, or several. Aside from those, Edgar's collection excited in me the strongest loathing. Those, and the ones in the shape of pug dogs. And the little banty roosters. My darling, my truer soul, my second spirit! You grew up wild as a bramble on the common, you never had such curios for your distraction. How they would have fallen to pieces under your rough fingers, how you would have strewn filbert shells everywhere, caring not for those who might be barefoot but of tenderer hide than yours, in which number I must include myself."

·

Heathcliff:

"Fiends of hell torment me at the memory! I recall the dull afternoon, the spinet dusty with disuse, and—ah!—Cathy's smooth and round hand holding that damned kickshaw of Linton's, although I should mention that the weapon the wretched huntsman in question aimed at the squirrel-infested stump was a crossbow, unmistakably, and nothing like a musket. I nearly took my blackthorn stick and smashed the thing to atoms, and the rest of the nutcracker menagerie in its belowstairs den or wherever it might be. I know he also had a few that went everywhere with him in the boot of his carriage, which he would haul out in one village or another and show to the populace, for what purpose I cannot tell, and those I wished to hurl beneath his wheels and scatter in splinters across the paving stones. Cathy, my Cathy! I hear the wild music of her voice, I see her graceful form as she operates that gadget, shelling nutmeats as the twilight descends, piling up far more than any ten people could eat.

"Write to me, ye ardor-starved hobbyists, Squire McEachern and your crew, and I'll commit your inky pages to my parlor fire, and warm my slippers with 'em. I crack nuts with my own strong back teeth, nothing more, or by stomping down with my bootheels, or hard in the crook of my right arm, if need be, and scoff at your mechanistical go-devils."

·

EPILOGUE:

Nutcracker fanciers did indeed take Mr. Heathcliff up on his challenge, and wrote to him in such numbers as to strain the local postal service. Rather than burning all the letters, Mr. Heathcliff read one or two at idle moments, then scratched a few brief responses, and thus began a lively correspondence with Mr. Ulrich Link, of Ulm, Germany, which went from enmity, to growing respect, and finally to warm friendship, which continues today.

Cathy died, but not seriously. Edgar Linton made the (for him) unprecedented decision to allow a portion of his collection to tour the Continent and the eastern United States, with stops in all the major cities. From the revenues received, he was able to purchase some unusual cigar trimmers seized from a tobacconist for nonpayment of tariff. After a reasonable period of mourning, he began to look for a companion whose interests more closely matched his own.

Issues and Non-issues

Summary: In May, the American Prosperity Foundation, Inc., an office-based sampling organization, chose from a preselected group a smaller group, which it believed was unusually significant. Then professionals took that subset and divided it even further. At issue was whether an issue was an issue or a non-issue. On certain issues/non-issues, disagreement was so small as to be statistically negligible. For example:

ISSUE	NON-ISSUE
My taxes	Your taxes

So far, so good. Other i/non-i inquiries, while less clear-cut, nevertheless fell within an acceptable margin of certainty—

I	NON-I
The Russian Suicide Death Chair	Regular chairs

where acceptable certainty was taken to be a percentage greater than sixty-six, or slightly more than

America's ninety-three million television households.

So far, so good. However, what were researchers to do in cases like the following?

I (NON-I)	NON-I(I)
"She's the Sheriff"	"Turner & Hooch"

If the first was designated an issue, although possibly not, in the judgment of many respondents, and the second was definitely not an issue except insofar as the first one was (albeit to a lesser degree), what then? The question seemed to lop the entire procedure off at the knees, and progress stalled.

Enter Nils Garrickson, a twenty-five-year-old wunderkind trained in the emerging science of cybernetics.

Unfortunately, he was fired, leaving us right back at square one. Then they brought in somebody else, Tom somebody. He also got fired. Then they brought in Marcie, who was more or less kicked upstairs from Accounting. What she did, first off, was to go through all the non-issues and take a whole new look just at them. She found, to her surprise, that many did not strictly qualify as non-issues at all, but included a sprinkling of pseudo-issues, sub-issues, secondary issues, meta-issues, and dead issues, as well as one or two real serious issues that had somehow been misfiled. Now we were getting somewhere. Printouts of the new, culled list of non-issues were issued to every department head. Marcie's managerial style was hands-on, direct, and at times confrontational. Part Welsh, part Greek, with a slight mustache and a big, strapping form, she got the most from her smaller male associates. First off, she established a standard of "i/non-i-ness," based on the following model:

I	NON-I
Golf junkets	Miniature-golf junkets

Later quantifying the standard by means of a simple algebraic formula (included in work sheet), she received the Nobel Prize.

At the time, my department was working on an issue for which we had not yet found a corresponding non-issue:

I	NON-I
Sex in the workplace	?

I had run through all the non-i tables without success, and Marcie was becoming impatient. One Easter I stayed over just to get some hours to myself on the computer. Monday morning rolled around and I hadn't had a chance to go home and shower. Suddenly it hit me! I ran into Marcie's office. She was watering her plants. She'd just arrived. Puzzled, she looked up as I scrawled on her blackboard:

Issues and Non-issues

I	NON-I
Sex in the	Sex in the
workplace	fireplace

Marcie plugged the coördinates into her formula—and, sure enough, they checked out. We examined our figures again and again to make absolutely certain. Overjoyed, we reviewed my data sheets to see if they contained any discoveries that might be patentable, and we found plenty.

From then on, everything seemed to happen at once. Funding poured in. People had been waiting for a system that could reliably provide non-issues for any issues that came up, and vice versa. Now we had that system in place, with an exclusive seventeen-year license worldwide. In short order, we were able to engineer the following i/non-i couplings:

I	NON-I
Scofflaw	Diplomats in
diplomats	general
Gangsta rap	Gangsta gift wrap
The B-1 bomber	The B-flat bomber
Young Elvis,	Old Elvis,
old Elvis	dead Elvis

Each of these produced revenues for the foundation well in excess of thirty-five hundred dollars. Everyone began to look forward to going to work in the mornings.

Staffers took each other out to lunch and splurged on health insurance. Every day, it seemed like, someone was coming up with a new "eureka" and shooting off a Roman candle in the commissary.

.

Then, one afternoon just before quitting time—we'd been getting along so well, and our system was working so beautifully!—Marcie fired me. The first thought that ran through my mind was, Never sleep with someone from the office! Of course, I hadn't slept with anyone, but that was small comfort now. As she turned to leave my cubicle and stepped into the hall, someone fired her. Then the guy who fired her heard his phone ringing and, when he picked it up, learned he had been fired. I cleaned out my desk and fired some people and went home, only to find a message on my machine from Personnel telling me I'd been re-hired. But that turned out to be an error: the next day I received official notification that I'd been fired.

Naturally, the stage was now set for Nils Garrick-son, Part Two. He was calling himself Nilsa and was taking a whole new approach. Apparently he/she had obtained some funds for a business to warehouse closed issues which technicians would then attempt to reopen. NilsCo offered me a flat daily rate, no benefits, everything off the books. Some of the issues I was working with were so closed that I was forced to resort to procedures which were bad science, even dangerous. Once or twice I managed to turn a closed issue into a fuzzy issue, but that was about it. After a few months, I quit.

•

I sat at home collecting unemployment and waiting for my phone to ring. Meanwhile, the world moved farther away from the old i/non-i classical polarities in which I had been trained. Some would say that it had never conformed to our model to begin with, and perhaps they would be right. The rare piecework assignments I picked up almost never involved a good textbook non-issue—just issues that someone wanted me to skirt or talk around.

Now, as I look back over my career, I realize that issues versus non-issues, as an issue, is something of a false issue. We all get caught up in discussion of the issues, and we try to use reason, and it's such a waste. Our country is being destroyed. Focussing on our differences blinds us to an evil that threatens everything we've worked for and cherish. In addition, we must try to develop a new mode that defines issues less in terms of what they are not (or are). This can sound more complicated than it really is, if only we break it down, which can be done easily by someone with the proper theoretical tools.

Line 46a

Dear Taxpayer:

As Commissioner of Internal Revenue, I would like
to take a moment to familiarize you with new tax laws
that will affect all those filing Form 1040, Schedules
A through SE. Please note that, as of this year, taxpayers filing single or joint returns are provided with
the option of checking one of two boxes on Line 46a.
(Miscellaneous Credits). You may check either the
box marked "Yes" in the first category or the box
marked "Yes" in the second category. If filing jointly,
your spouse must also check one of these two boxes.
Selection of a category is required of all taxpayers.

Frequently asked questions:

*What tax benefits will I receive if I check "Yes" in
the first category?*

Within thirty days, you will receive a mailing from
your local I.R.S. office, as a result of which you will
die. Should your death occur in a year in which you
already have tax liability, the anticipated decrease in
income will keep that liability close to the previous

amount. For this reason, taxpayers choosing the first category are encouraged to file early.

What if I check "Yes" in the second category? What happens then?

We realize that tax laws are complex and sometimes frustrating. In an effort to streamline bureaucratic procedures, we ask all who decide that the second category makes better tax sense for them to call one of several phone numbers listed on page 28 of the instruction booklet. A representative will record your Social Security number and describe a preselected individual or group of individuals to you. When the next filing deadline comes around, you will fill out your return as usual, indicate your eligibility for tax credit, and enclose check or money order payable to Internal Revenue Service. Be sure to list victim's name and taxpayer identification number on your payment.

How soon do I get my refund?

You'll get your refund soon enough—from four to eight weeks, depending on time of filing. You don't have to worry about that.

What if I am unable to choose a category on Line 46a? Are there any other options available to me?

No. As per Section 5 of the Choices Offered to Citizens by Government act, these choices are the only ones you have. In certain instances, preselected taxpayers may be able to choose both categories, but not for longer than one calendar year. If you are unable to choose, an I.R.S. representative will compute your choice for you.

Can I apply for an extension?

You or your tax preparer may, if unable to file by deadline, apply for an extension by submitting Form 4868, Application for Automatic Extension of Time (due April 15). An extension of four months may be granted, provided you have already chosen a category on Line 46a.

I'm single, live alone, and have no dependents.

Perfect. If you choose the first category, you will retain your one exemption (yourself) for that tax year regardless of the date on which your death occurs, as long as it is on or before December 31. If you choose the second category, you will be able to move about freely, store materials in your house or apartment, and amass a paper trail of deductible long-distance travel expenses, which will lower your tax bill still further. From a tax standpoint, you win either way.

What if I choose a category and then change my mind?

All taxpayers are permitted to file an amended return up until six months from the filing date, after which time their decision is regarded as final.

I'm a first-time filer. What if I miss?

Read Step 4, "How to Avoid Common Mistakes," found on page 9. It will assist you in important procedures, such as finding street addresses and calculating daily routine. If you need additional help, you may call your local I.R.S. office. (Note: To make sure that you receive deniable service, two or more I.R.S. representatives sometimes listen in on calls.)

The government—not just the United States of

America but the government in general—could not function without the voluntary compliance of millions of citizens like you. You deserve excellence in the service that we in the government provide. We understand your need for simplification and paperwork reduction. We, too, are ordinary taxpayers in most cases. Without your taxes and prompt selection of a category on Line 46a, we would not be able to do a number of things that the government has to do: provide essential social services; fund projects; build bridges, cul-de-sacs, and roads; and regulate interstate trade. In return, you have a right to expect that what happens to you will be applied fairly and across the board. We are reaching out to bring noncompliers back into the program, to insure that everyone does his or her part. We are vigorously pursuing enforcement of category choice, so that every citizen receives no fewer than two categories to choose from, and no more.

Our goal is full compliance from every citizen by the end of the decade. You will make this easier by filing voluntarily and without frivolous objection. Your decision, whatever it may be, will help us to see a little farther into the future, to a day when the government can do away with such necessities. Thank you again for making the only choice you can.

Dial W-H-Y W-O-R-K

Thank you for calling the No-Show Jobs Hotline. If you are interested in no-show or seldom-show employment with state, federal, or other agencies, and are calling from a rotary phone, please stay on the line and a representative will assist you. If you are calling from a touch-tone phone, please press "1."

If you are inquiring about the job as Part-Time Counsel to the State Assembly Committee on Federal-State Relations, you must first submit to a brief interview. Do you possess a valid degree from an accredited school? (If the answer is "yes," press "1.") Are you over the age of twenty-one? (If the answer is "yes," press "1.") Do you possess an answering machine? (If "yes," press "1.") Congratulations—you're hired! Salary checks will be issued on the first and fifteenth of every month, delivered to you by next-day express or wired directly to your bank account, as you request.

The following up-to-the-minute listing of unclaimed no-show jobs is provided courtesy of a friend of Janet's father's from when he was doing the books for the County Assessor's office:

Liaison to the Transportation Safety Committee. A plum no-show, ideal for boy- or girlfriend of higher-up government official. Some signing of documents required;

Secretary to the Special Counsel to the State Assembly. No typing, dictation, or other office chores mar this great free-ride opportunity. Twice-yearly semi-mandatory attendance at opening of legislative sessions calls for public servant with flexible schedule;

Administrative Director of the Temporary State Commission to Revise the Social Services Law. After-tax salary of $1,346 biweekly, plus pension and full health and dental, provides peace of mind, walking-around money;

Special Assistant to the Subcommittee on Transportation. Applicant must have knowledge of all surface routes from home to nearest cash machine. Proof of United States residency suggested;

Director of Government Operations for the State Senate Majority Leader. Duties include filing for personal parking space in State House Lot No. 1 and making occasional nuisance calls. Eighteen thousand per year, plus benefits;

Ten-Thousand-Dollar-a-Month Campaign Strategist (Unaffiliated). Payee may endorse compensation either with own name or "For deposit." Please note that space below endorsement line is for bank use only.

Planning a midweek getaway? No-show jobholders may take advantage of the lowest off-peak rates at resorts, hotels, and casinos. All you need is a paid associate to cover for you on the remote chance that something comes up, and the latest in sophisticated cellular call-forwarding. In addition, custom communication services such as Call Reversing and Automatic Call Disconnect can buy extra vacation time, should you wish it. The No-Show Jobs Hotline provides free travel arrangements in return for a small promotional announcement stuck on your airline seat back. Don't forget that you may be entitled to up to six weeks' paid vacation over and above vacations you take on your own. In most cases, the accounting department is required to cut those checks for you at the beginning of the paid vacation period, *before* the dates on which such payments would normally fall due. Unless you are watchful, office personnel may withhold money owed simply because they show up regularly and you don't. Get to know these people! Your ability to match first names with office extension numbers can mean the difference between prompt payment and an inconvenient trip downtown. Obtain a detailed office roster of accounting, payroll, and disbursement staffs and study it in your spare time. You may even wish to meet a few of the more important staffers in person when you happen to be in the neighborhood, on the way to or from the airport. Just because a job requires no effort doesn't mean it's going to be easy.

The Frankest

Interview Yet

A: I was having sex. I had had sex previously, found
that I enjoyed it, and so was having it again. With a
sexual partner, I screwed all over the floor. Orgasms
were multiple for the both of us. I took a lover, also.
Plus I had a tryst with a fellow in the shower room of
the old Grand Avenue Y. I turned an empty office at
work into a snuggery, and made use of it. I became
proficient not only in standard English, but also in
tavern English. I cursed like a sailor or sometimes
like a navvy. I mixed obscenities with profanities at
will when the spirit moved me, using anatomical and
physiological terms, inferences of parentage, and
blasphemies. When called upon, I could turn the air
blue.

Oral sex.

See what I mean? I did not (and do not) shrink from
explicit language. If you are shocked, or perhaps are
feeling ambivalent about what I am saying, good.
Sexual practices should be more open, and no one
knows this better than I. When the young shopgirls
in their sheer blouses and blank faces come ankling

into the elevator, my expression turns unmistakably sensual. I simply drip with sex. It oozes from my every pore, which I like, and they do, too. And when I see a strapping young hoss of a guy the experience is remarkably similar. I wiggle like a streetwalker and go right up to him and say, "Hello, my name is Mr. Bascom." I garden in the near-nude in the residential community where I live. I put on a pair of coveralls only when the weather is chilly or I'm doing landscaping. If my neighbors are offended, they shouldn't be. I have an excellent, heavyset body. We are all deeply sexual beings.

I met a young woman with a criterion figure and bedroom eyes at a sales event the other day. I mentally undressed her, then re-dressed her. She noticed the pertinacious quality of my stare, and asked, "What are you looking at, Mr. Johnsberry?" I mumbled a pleasantry and looked away. She knew as well as I did that if we wanted, we could screw. I could tell she was appraising me, wondering what I'd be like in the sack, and if I was a swordsman. I wouldn't have been at all surprised if she had a mental image of me bare-butt naked. So much the better. I informed her that my name was Mr. Bemis, and that I would very much enjoy her company in my hotel suite later in the evening. We began chatting. The sexual tension, undercurrents, and electricity in the air were so thick you could have seen them, while our colleagues leered at us with a casual knowingness.

Her name was Ms. Buxbaum, and Christ, what a great lay she turned out to be! After the obligatory postcoital cigarette, I immediately went to church and confessed my sins and was shriven for them, the peace of divine forgiveness filling me as I bent over the prayer rail in my fellow-congregants' holy, homely scent of soap and dry-cleaned wool and Sunday shoe polish. By the renewed light of the high chancel windows I signed my name, Mr. Randsworthy, in the registry. Then it was back to the hotel. My lover at the time was a male nurse, and you know how nurses are. He was lithe, sloe-eyed, and rather matter-of-fact about sex, as are many young men who work in hospitals. We discovered a mutual pursuit that gave us enormous pleasure: screwing our heads off.

Yes, I believe in lap dancing. Far from censuring it, I wholeheartedly encourage it as a healthy outlet. At the end of a long day, with my colleagues Mr. Pixley, Mr. Simpkins, et al., I often spend a few wickedly relaxing hours at a small club I know of where lap dancing is done. To have a well-built entertainer of either sex clad in little more than thong, pasties, and/or black bow tie sit in one's lap and gyrate has a marvellous effect. In this, of course, my views come into direct conflict with those of many. I believe that opposition to lap dancing is a destructive holdover from the Puritans, and have argued my point on a number of occasions, even with members of my own family—my children, and their spouses or companions. By now they know enough not to expect moralizing pabulum from me.

The children's mother, Ms. Frampton, and I had great sex throughout our long marriage and, quite candidly, before, when we were just a couple of randy college kids shacking up. In those days, Johnson (my pet name for my or any penis) could become an ivory wand virtually at command and achieve orgasm in just a few penile thrusts. Then, as now, I wore painted-on trousers with stirrups at the cuffs to pull them down even tighter, and my fiancée, Ms. Samples, did the same. We acquired a reputation on campus for unashamed and forthright behavior, which I have maintained ever since. All the kids except Gary know the time, place, and erotic circumstances of their conception, and are stronger for it. All the kids except Gary can tell you the particulars, thus freeing themselves and others from prudery and cant. When I heard that Gary was having problems at school, I flew up on the shuttle first thing the next morning, met with the Dean, Mr. Bentley, had sex, and thrashed out the whole situation. The following term, Gary's marks were back up where they belonged. Neither I, Gary's mother, nor his probable biological dad ever spared any effort with Gary, which is why I find some of his recent remarks unsubstantiated.

From the point of view of one who has spent the balance of his life pursuing vigorous sexual intercourse and sport-screwing, I can say that public attitudes have changed for the better. I give people like myself credit for this. How easy it would have been for me and my contemporaries to continue the back-stairs bundling and fondling and frottage that characterized earlier times. But I am an avowed hedonist and sensualist, whose lasting legacy will be more of the same. I don't care how the future may judge me, Mr. Spradlin, as long as it acknowledges that I chased after anything in a skirt or trousers and mounted and was mounted freely. The sexual response is a pleasure given by God, in most cases. To deny this is to deny a natural desire to hear about my sex life and the sex lives of thousands of other businesspeople no different from ourselves.

The Novel's

Main Character

The novel's hero . . . is the English language.
> —Dust-jacket quote

. . . The novel is about more than four lives; the bonds among the women . . . almost seem a character in their own right.
> —*New York Times Book Review*

The city of Dublin is the novel's main character.
> —Introduction to famous book

. . . Cicely, Alaska, is as much a central character as the individuals who inhabit it.
> —*TV Guide*

The main character is not the narrator but mortality itself.
> —*N.Y.T.B.R.*

Troy [New York] is the main character; it dominates the book.
> —*N.Y.T.B.R.*

. . . The novel is always about Bridgeport [Connecticut], which really is the central character.
> —*N.Y.T.B.R.*

New York City has been not only a backdrop for television series but a crusty character in its own right.
> —*The New Yorker*

The Novel's Main Character

The Bob [Marshall Wilderness Area] is more than
background; it's a character in the story.

—*Great Falls* (Montana) *Tribune*

"THE NOVEL'S MAIN CHARACTER"
A play in three acts
TIME: *The President*
PLACE: *Hedda Gabler*

Dramatis personae (in order of appearance):
The English Language .... Sir Ralph Richardson
The Bonds Among the Women ..... Sir John Gielgud
The City of Dublin .... Joan Plowright
Cicely, Alaska .... Claire Bloom
Mortality Itself .... Itself
Troy .... Kenneth Branagh
Bridgeport .... Kenneth Branagh
New York City .... Sally Kirkland
The Bob .... Dame Edith Evans

ACT I, SCENE I
Enter THE ENGLISH LANGUAGE, *in blue tights and
red cape.*

THE ENGLISH LANGUAGE:
          I before e, except after c,
          or when sounded as a,
          as in *neighbor* or *weigh.*

Enter THE BONDS AMONG THE WOMEN, THE
CITY OF DUBLIN, *and* CICELY, ALASKA, *in appropriate costumes.*

101

THE BONDS AMONG THE WOMEN (*in a loud whisper*): You're upstaging me, you know.

THE CITY OF DUBLIN: Oh, yeah? You almost-a-character, you! I oughta—

They fight.

CICELY, ALASKA: Help! Murder!

Enter MORTALITY ITSELF, in the form of a speeding tow truck, from stage right.

ALL: Save us!

CURTAIN.

ACT II, SCENE I

The lights come up to reveal TROY, *clad in black except for a headpiece representing the city skyline.*

TROY: I am Troy, a city of over fifty-four thousand, situated just minutes north of Albany. My principal industries are education, service, and local government.

Changes quickly to a headpiece representing BRIDGEPORT.

BRIDGEPORT: And I, in my valley of the Pequonnock, am substantial Bridgeport, proud employer of nearly two hundred thousand in the manufacture of transportation equipment, machinery, electrical equipment, fabricated metals, and other, nonspecified manufacturing.

Enter NEW YORK CITY, *in even fancier costume.*

NEW YORK CITY (*crustily*): Oh, shove it along, you scene-stealing, part-padding little—

Kicks him in shins.

BRIDGEPORT: Bloody hell!

Lunges at her. They grapple to the floor.

The Novel's Main Character

CURTAIN.

INTERMISSION.

ACT III, SCENE I

Enter THE BOB, *in an endless-mountainous-waste-of-snow-trees-and-sky costume.*

THE BOB: Created by act of Congress in 1966, I am the largest officially designated Wilderness Area in the contiguous forty-eight states. I can beat anybody.

Enter omnes. General free-for-all ensues.

MORTALITY ITSELF *crushes* TROY/BRIDGEPORT *under its wheels.*

THE BONDS AMONG THE WOMEN *and* THE CITY OF DUBLIN *stab each other.*

NEW YORK CITY *and* CICELY, ALASKA, *butt heads, fall unconscious.*

THE ENGLISH LANGUAGE *is killed attempting to intervene.*

None are left standing but MORTALITY ITSELF *and* THE BOB.

THE BOB: I am the land, I endure.

Fires a grenade launcher through MORTALITY IT-SELF'S *windshield.*

MORTALITY ITSELF *explodes in flames, siren screeching. Siren fades.*

CURTAIN.

·

"The Novel's Main Character" was first performed before a live audience in the Old Ben Theatre in London, England. Subsequently, a production featuring the original cast was mounted in New York, using a text in which a few words had been changed—"lorry" to "flashlight," for example—to make it more acceptable to an American ear. Critics agreed that no cast could have better suited the roles. As The English Language, Sir Ralph invested the part with shadings that gave the audience a sense of what it felt like to be a modern language from the inside; at the character's tragic and unnecessary death in Act III, some had to look away. Sir John, departing from typecasting to play The Bonds Among the Women, fleshed out the role beautifully with expressive hand gestures. The supporting players—Mmes. Plowright and Bloom—did all that could be asked, despite their relatively brief stage time, while Miss Kirkland and Mr. Branagh portrayed large metropolitan areas with aplomb. The evening, however, belonged to Dame Edith as The Bob, who always brought the house down with her entrance, carrying her costume as lightly as if it were silk and not a two-hundred-pound construction of dentist's plaster, model-railroad evergreens, and artificial snow. After a long run on Broadway, the company toured the States, and then the play became a popular radio show, a movie, and then a play again, with a different title but the same idea. Many of the original cast members went on to newfound fame in their adopted country in a variety of stage and screen roles. Dame Edith, a victim of her own success, grew tired of always being cast as scenery, and so returned home.

Your Face or Mine

WE CAN KICK YOUR CITY'S ASS
—*New slogan for New York City, proposed on a TV
show, embraced by Mayor Giuliani, and offered as a
button from the New York* Daily News

First thing every morning when I sit down to eat, I
get in my breakfast's face. I violate the space of that
breakfast—the dry cereal, one-per-cent skim, fruit
juice, what have you—I really get loud with it. I tell
it what I want it to do for me that day from a nutritional
standpoint. Hey, I'm a New Yorker—my food doesn't
give *me* ulcers, I give *it* ulcers. Then I eat it. I go at
that breakfast one hundred per cent. And I don't care
what you're havin', eggs over, hash browns, grits like
they got down South (grits! what a joke!), my breakfast
can kick whatever you're havin' 's ass. It's not what's
on the plate, it's the attitude. With the right New York
attitude, I can take my breakfast and beat your breakfast, then take your breakfast and beat my breakfast.

A word of warning here, in case you're thinking
that because I get in my breakfast's face you can just
come up and get in *my* face. Think twice about that,
my friend. You want to get in my face, take a number.
Let me explain: I'm a New Yorker, so naturally I'm
not going to hear you unless you get in my face. In
fact, I restrict myself exclusively to in-your-face peo-

ple, places, and things, because that's the way I like it. Unfortunately, there's just one problem. Recently, I measured my face, and I don't think I've got more than about seventy square inches of surface area there. Think about it: not a lot of room. The *Daily News* gets in my face every morning, and that more than fills my face right there. So I guess, loving this ass-kicking city as I do, what I really need is a hell of a lot bigger face.

The other day, I went ballistic, which I like to do. We—some fellow New Yorkers and I—were out kicking some other cities' asses. We started in Jersey, on the bank of the Hudson, and worked our way south. First we kicked Englewood's ass, then we kicked Englewood Cliffs' ass, then Fort Lee's ass, then Ridgefield's ass. I mean, we were taking no prisoners. Suddenly, I got distracted, and as we were kicking the ass of North Bergen I inadvertently took some prisoners. Dumb mistake. Now I got all these prisoners chained to the fence in the twenty-four-hour parking lot across the street. It so happens that my friend Bill lives, or lived, in North Bergen. Now the guy is yelling at me from the lot every morning, "So, you kicked our city's ass! Big deal! In New York, you got—what?—eight, nine million people? In North Bergen we got forty-eight thousand four hundred and fourteen, counting my wife and me. How fair is that?" He just doesn't understand. I don't care about fair. Fair is for horseshoes and hand grenades, whatever that means. I don't play nothin' I can't win, and I don't win nothin' I can't etc. Help me out, here, Shirley!

Your Face or Mine

Luckily for me and others, I work as hard as I play. Weekdays, I'm all business. But come Friday I strip off the coat and tie and Merry Widow waist-cincher corset, and change into baggy sweatshirt, jeans, and heels. Then it's down to the playground for an arms-and-elbows game of big-city asphalt-court basketball. In my game, there are two rules: (1) No blood, no foul; and (2) It's not over till the other guys lose. Which, to be up front about it, they always do. I drive on my opponents, I fake them out of their shoes, I stuff them like a Christmas turkey. My game's butter and they're toast, and the only way they're ever going to check me is if they check my groceries at A. & P. If they are smaller and weaker than I am, I flatten them, but if they are my size or bigger—hey, I'm not too proud to back off. I sort of shuffle and bow down, sometimes all the way to their sneaker tops, to let them know I'm making a sincere effort here. Afterward, in my apartment, suddenly something comes over me and I kick my own ass. Hey, it happens, it's nothing I can help. My doctor says it's a medical condition. Unlike most people, due to my specific metabolism, I do need the aggravation. *Kick! Ouch! Kick! Ouch!* I'm writhing around like a carp here. But I'm a New Yorker: I scream and I yell, but then I hug and I kiss. My foot says it's sorry, and makes up with my ass, and my ass accepts the apology, and we all go out for coffee and Danish. I eat standing at the counter in the toughest city in the world.

Making "Movies"

in New York

If you live in New York City, or if you've ever visited it, you have probably come across street locations where movies are being made. There are big motor homes parked at the curb, and equipment trucks, and cables on the sidewalk, and brisk young people with polo shirts and walkie-talkies asking you please to walk on the other side. For me, as for most New Yorkers, such an occurrence is now commonplace, and I obey the brisk young people without a thought. Or, rather, I used to. Recently I have made a strange discovery: whatever it is those "film crews" are really doing with their clipboards and their umbrella reflectors and their streetside buffet tables and their hand-lettered signs saying MAKEUP or WARDROBE or MR. VARNEY'S TRAILER, *they're not making movies!*

This discovery came about by coincidence. Some years ago I took my sister and two of her friends for drinks in a bar in the lobby of a midtown hotel. We had hardly begun our first round when the waiter told us that we would have to leave, because someone was about to begin filming a movie there. Suddenly squads of brisk young people were toting cables and moving furniture and talking among themselves in a telegraphic way. As we slid toward the revolving doors, I managed to ask one of them what movie they were working on. He mentioned the name of a well-known director and the title: *They All Laughed.*

That should have tipped me off right there. Instead, I watched the movie pages of the local papers for months, then years, waiting for the opening of *They All Laughed.* Of course, any well-informed person knows that probably there is not and never has been any such movie. *They All Laughed?* I'll say they did. They probably howled and roared in the privacy of that emptied-out hotel bar, as they achieved whatever mysterious purpose they had commandeered it for. I began to think back over all the movies I had ever seen—could I name even one that had been filmed in New York? Also, I recalled other instances in which I had asked "film crews" the titles of the alleged movies they were working on. Once, a couple of large men blocking the entrance to the Brooklyn Bridge told me that it was closed for the filming of a movie called *Hudson Hawk.* Give me a break! *Hudson Hawk?* I could come up with a likelier title off the top of my head. And it goes without saying that no cinematic offering by that name ever did appear (as far as I know) at my local quadriplex. Another time, I couldn't eat at a favorite lunch counter downtown because of the purported filming of a supposed work titled *Something Wild.* In later years did I or anyone I know ever see or hear of the release of any movie by that name?

Well, maybe there was one, but I never ran across it. Sometimes I wonder why those "filmmakers" bother to concoct names for their "movies" at all.

.

So what *are* they up to, if they're not making movies? One rather obvious answer comes immediately to mind. They spend a lot of time in and near large motor homes—a favorite recreation of Californians. They move about the city from place to place; Californians are known for their mobility. Many of them are tan. They like to set up buffet tables in the out-of-doors —a habit reminiscent of the patio-style dining favored in California. The food on the buffet tables is usually juices, fresh fruit, and vegetables—well-known staples of the Californian diet. In short, these self-described "on-location crews" may simply be Californians who have adapted to the environment of New York City.

Naturally, the disguise of filmmaker suits these people better than it would emigrants from other states; California has long been known for its association with the movies. Still, I cannot help wondering if something more is going on behind the charade. A while ago the motor homes and cables and buffet tables showed up in my neighborhood in Brooklyn. This time crew members handed out flyers asking residents of certain streets to remove all air-conditioners from streetside windows, in the interests of the period authenticity of the "movie." Residents who failed to comply at once were petitioned again and again. My neighbors and I all took down our air-conditioners and laid them on the floor, where we tripped over and stubbed our toes on them for several days until a second flyer came telling us we could put them back. Meanwhile, the motor homes sat at the curbs with their cables snaking down into the basements of adjacent buildings. After a few days I noticed that the motor homes had gotten slightly larger, while the buildings they were connected to had lost a few feet in height.

On a hunch, I called Con Ed. They still haven't called me back, but when they do, I am sure another piece of the puzzle will be revealed. Meanwhile, I continue to watch the situation closely, and I advise others to do the same. Peek through a side window of the longest motor home the next time you come across a convoy parked somewhere. Most likely the shades will be tightly drawn. But if they aren't, chances are that this is what you'll see: feet in expensive running shoes, propped on a countertop or table; ankles, negligently crossed, in white sweat socks; tan bare shins covered with fine blond hairs; boxy tan knees; and, propped on the knees, an open copy of the New York *Post*. Many times I have seen just this sight bathed in the motor home's interior glow and framed in the porthole-like window. The brand of the running shoes may change, and the stripe on the sweat socks, and the issue of the newspaper, but the knees, the shins—they are always the same. Owing to the angle and perspective, I can never see the rest of the figure. It could be a woman; it is more

probably a man. The shins especially radiate an unmistakable aura of power. Unless I miss my guess,
they are the still center of the whole mad enterprise.
Something about them is tantalizingly familiar. If I
could match them with a face, perhaps I would know
all.

Stalin's Chuckle

Seldom did anyone see Stalin laugh. When he did, it
was more like a chuckle, as though to himself.

—G. Zhukov, Marshall of the Soviet Union,
Reminiscences and Reflections

Irwin C. Brown,
TV and Radio Entertainers' Retirement Home
Stalin's dacha, his summer place or whatever—now,
that was a hard room. I worked it just the one time
when I was on my world tour in the fifties. No stage
or nothin', only a little, like, conference table with a
lectern. I pushed the lectern aside, didn't need that
for my act. They offered me some herring, but herring
dries up my pipes. I just started right in. They was
all sittin' there, right in the front row. Matter of fact,
it was the only row, these big high-backed chairs:
Beria, Khrushchev, Poskrebyshev, Litvinov, Molotov.
Stalin sat on the aisle. Kept his hat on. I thought I
saw the mustache go up when I did my "Go get yourself
your *own* white man!" It just sort of went up, oh, 'bout
a quarter inch. That room was quiet, man. I could
see Beria holdin' it in, face turnin' purple. And Molotov was makin' these little chokin' sounds, kinda
snortin' out the nose every once in a while. But if Joe
don't laugh, don't *nobody* laugh.

Freddie Drake, Friars Club

I worked ten days at the old Flamingo in Las Vegas and then flew straight to Moscow. A. N. Poskrebyshev, the personal secretary, booked me. They put me up in a God-awful hotel, hot and cold running soot. At eleven at night some guy called for me and took me to the private apartment in the Kremlin where Stalin stayed when he couldn't get home. A lot of guys were sitting around with cigars and wine. It was a smoker, basically. I took one look and told myself, "Freddie, tonight you work blue." I used material so adult it would have gotten me kicked off American TV for life. Stalin was tanked but he didn't show it. I did the Shorty's joke, I did "Run, Harold, Run!," I did "Death or Chi-Chi"—nothing. I ended with my killer, really hit the punch line hard: "So the plumber says, 'I can save your wife, Mr. Schonstein—*but I'm afraid it's too late for the rabbi!*' " Stalin wanted to laugh, I know that. He did laugh, sort of, in that there was possibly a slightly redder color in his face. He gave off a strong feeling as if he might have been laughing. But did he *laugh* laugh? Not per se, no.

A. N. Poskrebyshev,
Palace of Party Members, Moscow

I remembered he used to play Allan Sherman's "Hello Muddah, Hello Faddah!" over and over again on the phonograph. This story-song of the young boy's letter home from summer camp made him helpless with laughing. Sometimes his mustache would rise perhaps half a centimetre. As his personal secretary, I had the job of replacing the needle at the beginning of each recording after it had reached the end. He especially liked the song "God Rest You, Gary Mandelbaum," and sometimes you would think he was almost humming along. Many other so-called novelty songs from America had a similarly strong effect on him. He often spoke of his desire to meet the man who wrote the song "I'm My Own Grandpaw."

Kayla T., Los Angeles
As a humor therapist, I immediately got a sense that all these men at the Kremlin were very stiff and rigid, and that uninhibited laughter might break up the rigidity—as it so often does. So I had the idea of getting everybody on the floor for a game of Ha. Now, in Ha what you do is you lie on the floor on your back, and somebody lies on his back perpendicular to you and rests his head on your stomach, and so on across the floor in sort of a herringbone pattern, and then the first person says "Ha," and the second person says "Ha, ha," and the third person is supposed to say "Ha, ha, ha," and so on. And the way your head bobs up and down on the other person's stomach when he says "Ha," it generally has everybody laughing hysterically by the time you get to three "Ha"s. I laid them out carefully—Mr. Molotov, Mr. Beria, Mr. Malenkov, and the others, with Mr. Stalin at the end. I told them all to relax and take deep breaths. Then Mr. Molotov said "Ha." Mr. Beria, suppressing giggles, continued with "Ha, ha." Mr. Malenkov strained to control his dignity as he added his "Ha, ha, ha."

Mr. Khrushchev's attempt at "Ha, ha, ha, ha" became an uncontrollable fit of belly laughs, which violently bounced Mr. Mikoyan's head, causing him to laugh until he wept, which in turn set off Mr. Yagoda. In a minute the whole line was howling with nonstop laughter—all except Mr. Stalin. His head bounced and bounced on his neighbor's stomach, but his expression didn't change. He stood, excused himself, and walked over to the men's room. He closed the door and slid the bolt. Gradually his colleagues on the floor began to calm down, and one by one they sat up. Soon we all fell completely silent. From the men's room we heard a faint sound. I am of the belief that what we heard was Mr. Stalin chuckling as though to himself.

A. N. Poskrebyshev

Booking comedy acts added greatly to my secretarial responsibilities, and I often neglected it in favor of more regular tasks. Comrade Stalin noticed this, imprisoned my wife, Bronislava, and then asked me to obtain at all costs a performance by a Mexican comedian. Through our embassy in Mexico City, I got in touch with ex-Comrade Trotsky, who was living there at the time. As it happened, Trotsky knew the Mexican comedy circuit well and had even contributed a few gags to some of its leading members. So in a manner of speaking certain comedians owed Trotsky a favor, and here was a perfect opportunity to make use of it. I was delighted with all these developments, and did not conceal my pleasure from

Comrade Stalin. At the mention of Comrade Trotsky's name, however, Comrade Stalin grew agitated and began to chuckle, as though to himself. Still chuckling, he insisted that I telephone immediately to Comrade Beria at his flat and summon him. When Beria arrived, Stalin rushed to the door, answered it, chuckled again, and screamed at Beria for his slowness. Chuckling very loudly as though to himself, he pushed Beria before him into the inner office and slammed the door. Soon after this he told me he would prefer to be entertained only by comedians from cold countries. "A Finn, for example, is always funny," he advised.

Though others may disagree, I have always maintained that Comrade Stalin knew funny. Hidden among his many attributes was a sure comedic sense. "You must never forget," he exhorted me, "a comic is one who says things *funny*, while a comedian is one who says funny *things*. Both of these phases, however, must be passed through on the way to the third and final phase: good stand-up. When we as a society attain really good stand-up, every evening will be open mike and the state as we know it will wither away. For jokes, we will require new ones appropriate to our modern times, and on modern themes—airplane food, for example, that syphilitic abomination! Or how about the vapid and syphilitic listings of television programs published in the newspapers? Such a form, if used in proper satiric style, could be most effective. A master of stand-up should possess a full repertoire of funny voices—Negro, sports announcer, and robot, to name only a few. Draw your comedy from daily life if you wish to reach the true audience: the people. Enough of the syphilitic vaudevillians' noise! The modern comedian will instead find his subjects at airports, in the behavior of overbearing shop clerks, and in the differences between one's own city and Los Angeles. Let us develop a scientific system for the production of trenchant comedy riffs, using as our models the best comedians of the past. Let our youngsters who wish to perform stand-up devote hours, years, to the watching of films of these masters. The true comic is the revolutionary, sticking swords in the stuffed shirts of the bourgeoisie. Let the comedy revolution never end, let it fill entire television channels, let it grow until everything is thoroughly funny!"

Eventually Comrade Stalin began to question my own sense of humor, and I was dismissed from his service. My wife, Bronislava, remained in prison until she was shot, I believe. Toward the end, the splendid theories of comedy Comrade Stalin had developed were under attack. Saddened as I was by his treatment of my wife and me, I did not lose faith in the soundness of these theories. Properly applied, they could have provided uproarious material on an international scale for years to come. The noise resembling a chuckle that we delighted to hear from Comrade Stalin's lips could have spread to every land. But, unfortunately for the cause of world humor, such a result was not to be.